ADVANCE PRAISE

What Coaches are Saying...

Coach Tom Anstett and Coach Tom McCormack are equal to any of the "big time" and celebrated college and NBA coaches we watch on television. Tom and Tom are "trenchers." Because they have both dedicated their entire lives to coaching high school boys in the "trenches," they may not be household names. Reading Victory Is in the Details *will show you why they should be. Having witnessed firsthand both Tom Anstett and Tom McCormack coach their respective high school programs has made me a better coach, and more importantly, so proud...that I am a Coach!!!*

~Douglas Bruno
Head Women's Basketball Coach
DePaul University (Chicago, IL)
USA Senior National Women's Team Assistant Coach (2008-2016)
USA 18 and 19-Year Old National Women's Team Head Coach (2006-2007)

Tom Anstett and Tom McCormack have been utilizing their tremendous basketball coaching skills to positively impact people for many years. They have done it again with this inspiring and motivational book, Victory Is in the Details. *Even now, as a college head coach and many years removed from playing high school basketball in Illinois, I can still remember being keenly aware of the passion these two coaches had for teaching the game the right way and getting their players to perform to the maximum of their potential. The information in this book will help both the veteran coach looking to sustain success and the new coach trying to build a culture of excellence. In addition, it is a must read for players who want to elevate their game and parents who want to support and encourage their sons or daughters in a positive and healthy way. After 30 years of coaching college basketball, I have come to realize that there are certain coaches who just "get it." Coach Anstett and Coach McCormack are two of those coaches, and we are all lucky that they have shared their wisdom in this fantastic book.*

~Brian Gregory
Head Men's Basketball Coach
University of South Florida (Tampa, FL), 16 years
Overall Record 296-233

The book is great and is a super valuable resource for all coaches at any level to help them institute what it takes to be successful.

~Patrick Ambrose
Head Coach of the Illinois 4A State Champion in 2015
Current Coach, Adlai E. Stevenson High School (Lincolnshire, IL)

Victory Is in the Details is a great read for any coach or even player regardless of level. I could tell within the first few pages that Tom and Tom are not only great coaches, but also great educators. The book breaks down a number of areas that will lead to individual and more importantly, team success. As a head college coach at the D-III level for 17 years, I've overlooked or forgotten many things within this book that will help make me a better coach.

~Gary Grzesk
Head Men's Basketball Coach
St. Norbert College (DePere, WI)
274-86 in 14 years
9 Midwest Conference Championships with 7 NCAA-Div. III Bids

Whether starting a basketball program or reviving one that has become stagnant, this book provides the wisdom of two outstanding high school coaches who will set you in the right direction. Respected for decades by the basketball community in Illinois for their integrity, hard work, ingenuity, and persistence, Tom Anstett and Tom McCormack team-up to share their wealth of basketball knowledge. Their collaborative efforts result in a manifesto of sorts that you will refer to frequently to build your portfolio of drills, develop your philosophy of offense and defense, and shape your perspective on how to teach the game...so, whatever the outcome on the scoreboard, you will be proud to call yourself a basketball coach. Reading this book will be the best call you make all season!

~Rich Kolimas
Current Head Boys' Basketball Coach
Lincoln-Way East High School (Frankfort, IL)

I look forward to getting a copy of the book upon its release. The acronym P-R-O-G-R-A-M provided many thought-provoking ideas that will help me evaluate my own program. So many great coaching nuggets and bullet points that coaches can use at all levels.

~Scott Trost
Head Men's Basketball Coach
Lewis University (Romeoville, IL)
23-Year College Head Coach,
Overall Record 412-241

Victory Is in the Details is so appropriate for these two tremendous authors, Tom Anstett and Tom McCormack. It is all about P-R-O-G-R-A-M with these two coaches. For many years I watched both compete at the highest level of high school basketball in Illinois. Both won at a very high level. But the thing I personally remember about Tom and Tom's teams were how hard their teams played and how fundamentally sound each team was both individually and as a team, regardless of how talented their teams were in that particular year.

Regardless if you are a coach, a player, or just a fan, this book will be an incredible read, containing so many stories behind the story. Dive into the minute details into becoming a better player, team, coach, or even person, how hard you have to prepare and work to be successful, and how to be honest with those in your program. Doing exactly what this book describes will make you better, regardless of your talent.

This upcoming season will be my 44ᵗʰ in coaching. I've coached every level: high school, NBA, and now at the college level, and I have been fortunate to win at every level. Hopefully, I have made a difference in many people's lives. But one thing I do believe is that what is in this outstanding book, if seriously read and studied, will make you the absolute Best You Can Be!

~Brian James
Men's Assistant Basketball Coach
Northwestern University Wildcats (Evanston, IL)
18-year NBA Coach with 5 Teams with at least 5 Hall of Fame Players
Illinois Basketball Coaches Hall of Fame Inductee

This read is an outstanding compilation of the wisdom of two outstanding Illinois scholastic Hall of Fame coaches. Both Coach McCormack and Coach Anstett have always been about how to best take care of kids and how to best grow the game of basketball. Their efforts here will definitely educate and inspire you to better serve your student-athletes and people in general with the tremendous life lessons that they share.

~Jim Tracy
Executive Director
Illinois Basketball Coaches Association

Victory Is in the Details *is an inspiring read. As coaches we can sometimes look past the details, and this book reminds us of their importance. Details matter and establish habits of play. The many areas that are discussed in this book will help build a strong foundation for your program.*

~Brian Wardle
Head Men's Basketball Coach
Bradley University (Peoria, IL)
Overall College Record 176-151

I have known Tom Anstett and Tom McCormack for nearly 40 years: we worked summer camps together, coached against each other, and spent countless hours thinking Xs and Os. Most of all, we built an enduring friendship. It was my honor to read a pre-release copy of their magnum opus: Victory Is in the Details. *As expected, this book contains dozens of ideas that both the rookie and veteran educator-coach can add to their coaching tool-boxes. Profoundly insightful and full of practical wisdom, this book is a "must" for every coach's library. Like its authors, it's a big winner!*

~Will Rey
Current Head Boys' Basketball Coach
Northridge Prep (Niles, IL)
313-151 in 16 seasons
Illinois Basketball Coaches Hall of Fame
Chicago Catholic League Inductee
(43-Year Career)

Victory Is in the Details *is a must read for any coach who wishes to develop and main-tain a championship program with a winning culture. This book is a unique combination of addressing the "why" of coaching in the big picture while also presenting the details, the "how," necessary to implement a successful program. Tom and Tom freely share the wisdom they have gained through many years of successful high school coaching experi-ence. I recommend this read for both beginning and veteran coaches as it is an invaluable resource for reaching one's potential as a coach.*

~Bob Williams
Former Head Coach
Schaumburg High School (Schaumburg, IL)
Illinois State Champion in 2001

Former Head Coach
Niles West High School
40-Year Career

Many books have been written with the promise of revealing how to build a successful basketball program and team. Tom Anstett and Tom McCormack have actually delivered. Victory Is in the Details *is a terrific treasure of basketball wisdom. These two outstanding coaches share their knowledge of coaching and teaching that they have gathered over a combined 92 years of experience. This book offers a profound understanding of what it takes to build a successful basketball program. Coaches at any level will value the attention to detail in this book and the valuable knowledge that can literally be put into practice in their own programs. Having coached against both men, I am not surprised that Anstett and McCormack have produced another winner with this book.*

~Rob Judson
Men's Assistant Basketball Coach
Marquette University Golden Eagles (Milwaukee, WI)
Illinois Basketball Coaches Hall of Fame Inductee, 1990

As a high school athlete, I competed against Coach McCormack's and Coach Anstett's teams. I always thought they were so physically and mentally tough. After now coaching collegiately for 30 years, I understand that so much goes into a team to be able to possess those traits. These two Hall of Fame coaches have provided a practical blueprint to develop a winning culture and championship mentality. A tremendous book for coaches at all levels!

~Porter Moser
Head Men's Basketball Coach
Loyola University (Chicago, IL)
NCAA Final Four, 2018

I have known Coach Tom Anstett since our playing days at Boston College. Although he was an outstanding roundball player, he was even better as a coach in the Chicago area. I have relied on his player evaluations for the Chicago area since 1973 when I got into the scouting profession. His unique ability to judge talent is due to his playing and coaching experiences. The quality I admire most about Coach Anstett is his ability to get the most out of his players on the court and in the classroom. That passion transfers to this book—a must read for all coaches at all levels.

~Rick Bolus
High Potential Blue-Chip Camp and Recruiting Service
(Shepherdsville, KY)

Tom Anstett and Tom McCormack have been two eminently successful coaches in the Chicago area. In this book they give readers 92 years of coaching experience in how to build a basketball program. Victory Is in the Details *should be on every coach in the country's reading list because it contains hundreds of practical insights into building a program. I only wish this outstanding book had been available while I was still coaching. It would have helped me immensely in my building programs at both the high school and collegiate levels.*

~Pat Sullivan
(Retired) Head Men's Basketball Coach
The University of St. Francis (Joliet, IL)
Member of 8 Halls of Fame

I started this book already having great respect for both Coach McCormack and Coach Anstett; if possible, I have even more admiration for them after reading it. It's evident why they were both so successful in coaching after reading firsthand about their methods for running and sustaining great programs. This book will help coaches who want to learn about proven techniques that will help them achieve more at all points in their careers. It's a resource that not only was I able to take many ideas and thoughts from, but also a book that I wouldn't hesitate to recommend to others.

~Gene Heidkamp
Current Head Boys' Basketball Coach
Benet Academy (Lisle, IL)
291-82 in 12 Seasons

Having played for four years in a program under these two coaches, I can vouch for the consistency, discipline, commitment, and fundamentals they taught and expected from their players. There was no "one set of rules for the standout players and another set for the rest." It was all about the team, thinking of the other person, and the actions impacting overall team productivity. Everyone mattered and bought in. The results spoke for themselves. I look forward to reading the book and after watching several years of high school basketball with my sons in different programs, I wish they could have played for Coach Anstett or Coach Mac. For you young coaches out there, garner all you can from this duo.

~Frank Gregorio
Former Player
Immaculate Conception High School
Class of 1984 (Elmhurst, IL)

DREAM

DEVELOP

COMPETE

WIN

VICTORY IS IN THE DETAILS

VICTORY IS IN THE DETAILS

BUILDING A BASKETBALL PROGRAM

Tom Anstett

Tom McCormack

VICTORY IS IN THE DETAILS
Building a Basketball Program

Windy City Publishers
2118 Plum Grove Road, #349
Rolling Meadows, IL 60008

www.windycitypublishers.com

Published in the United States of America

ISBN#:
978-1-953294-02-9

Library of Congress Control Number:
2020919868

WINDY CITY PUBLISHERS
CHICAGO

To our loving, supportive, and inspirational wives:
Susan Anstett and Mary Alis McCormack.

Thank you.
Love you.

CONTENTS

Good—better—best—

Never—never—rest—

Till the good is better—

And the better BEST!

~St. Jerome

# AUTHORS' NOTE

BASKETBALL COACHES AND PLAYERS WHO buy and study this book might assume they will learn more about coaching and playing this fantastic game. We know they are correct in that assumption. There is no money-back guarantee coming with that brash statement, but we feel confident their brains will be stoked with lots of fuel for their upcoming seasons. This confidence stems from our combined 92 years of basketball coaching.

For the experienced coaches of ten years or more, reading another book about basketball might fall into the feeling of watching a favorite movie for the tenth time. During the movie, you know what is coming, but think, "I never quite realized that," or "I knew I was on the right track, but that concept reaffirms…," or "I had never discussed that…with my player(s)." Thus, readers can realize tweaks and improvements in the details for their coaching and will be anxious to use them in the upcoming season. And yes, they will read the book again and might even start a dialogue with one or both of the authors. Moreover, the veteran coaches will find this book reinforces what they are already doing well and stay the course, especially when the waters get rough. In short, the longer coaches stay on the sidelines, the more those individuals realize what they have to learn or ways they can discover new approaches and instructional methods for their athletes. On the other hand, we do not expect readers to agree with everything in this book, but those contrasts offer healthy thinking.

The less experienced coaches of fewer than ten years, those in their first year of coaching, or those unaware of Hubie Brown or Rick Majerus have selected this book because perhaps it was given to them by a wise head coach or a friend or just want to learn more. These coaches know they have much to learn and, more importantly, possess an unquenchable thirst, similar to Clint Eastwood's march through the desert in The Good, The Bad, and the Ugly. Of course, Clint was being held at gunpoint for that suffering, but sometimes coaches need that extra push. As they read, they will be stuck on certain parts, investigating and/ or questioning the details for their own programs and abilities and will return to reading at every opportunity. If these coaches in this group are married, they will find every opportunity to read; if they are single, they might even consider skipping a night out to continue the reading.

Although coaches are the primary audience for this book, players might also partake, at least those players who desire greatness and improvement. They will put down their headphones and read this book to see the various factors that drive coaches crazy. On the other hand, they will realize the motivation and techniques that good coaches give to them for their own games. Players will acquire a more thorough understanding of both the difficulties and the rewards in a coaching life. Through those understandings, they will add to their own abilities, realizing the degree to which mind power is essential for being a good player. Players might even appreciate their mentors even more. Perhaps another view of the movie Hoosiers is in order; hopefully, that viewing will not be the first time they have seen it.

~Tom and Tom

(l. to r.) Tom McCormack, Tom Anstett (1978 relic)

FOREWORD

COACHING IS TEACHING, COACHING IS LEADING. A successful athletic program requires a leader with vision, character, competence, courage, mental toughness, and people skills. Building and maintaining a successful athletic program are challenges that all head coaches face, regardless of their sport. It starts with the understanding that the culture of a program should be built on mutual trust and respect and built through actions. The foundation of a program should be the core values and character of all members.

I have had an opportunity in my career to observe, listen to, and learn from many outstanding coaches and leaders in athletics. These people not only built strong programs but also impacted the lives of their players for the better because of their positive leadership. Throughout my forty years as a coach, Tom Anstett and Tom McCormack are two of the best coaches I have known in the high school arena. I watched their teams play and have coached against them in their Hall of Fame careers. We have spent countless hours together exchanging ideas about drills, strategies, or life in general. I consider them trusted friends, but I also know them as adversaries on the court. Coach Anstett was the head coach at three different schools, each school belonging to a very competitive conference in all sports. In that time, I had the opportunity to coach against his teams in nine non-conference games. Coach McCormack, on the other hand, was in the same conference as my school, and we played his teams 28 times. If my team earned the victory, we had to be at our best because their teams did not beat themselves.

Needless to say, throughout all our times together, I learned a great deal about Coach Anstett and Coach McCormack and about the values their programs modeled. Some of these values were:

- Their teams were ready to compete and were well coached.

- Their players were taught to be interchangeable on both offense and defense.

- They inspired their athletes to believe in themselves.

- They set themselves to the highest standards and led by example.

- Their programs were built on respect, trust, hard work, grit, and selflessness.

- They empowered their athletes to succeed.

- They used basketball as the vehicle to teach life lessons.

- They developed character and such core values as honesty, integrity, work ethic, responsibility, accountability, maturity, mental toughness, and positivity in their players.

- The practice structure, drills, expectations, attention to detail, and their teaching skills empowered their teams to play hard, play smart, and play together.

Victory Is in the Details is a well-planned, well written, and thought-provoking book. The authors have a combined 92 years of teaching and coaching athletes from grade school through high school where they taught players how to become the best they could be, empowering them to succeed while inspiring them to believe in themselves. This book is a must-read for coaches of all levels and experience. In it you will learn the What, the Why, and the How of program building. Coach Anstett and Coach McCormack do an excellent job of highlighting their thoughts, their drills, and their knowledge of teaching and coaching the game of basketball.

~Ed Molitor, Sr.
Illinois Basketball Coaches Hall of Fame inductee, 1997

Champion "Shoot-the-Bull" squad in 1992
(l. to r.) John Siwicki, Tom McCormack, Tom Anstett, Ed Molitor

PREFACE

WHAT ARE A FEW THINGS every basketball coach can understand? Coaching is hard. Coaching is frustrating. Coaching is challenging. Coaching requires many hats. Coaching offers some of the most uplifting moments in life. Make your own selection. Both of us discovered all of the above early in our careers. Ironically, the toughest moments were the ones that glued us to the many years on various sidelines.

 REFLECTION

TOM ANSTETT

I walked into a boys' locker room of downcast sophomores in December of 1973, my first year of coaching boys' basketball, after my team lost 82-22 at St. Benedict High School. You read right. A 60-point defeat, but slaughter was more appropriate. There is an old saying applied to athletics and to life: "You are not as bad as the day of your worst defeat, nor are you as good on the day of your greatest victory. You are somewhere in the middle." I hoped that statement was accurate because at that moment I wanted to cherish any middle. After wiping my eyes and regaining any remaining composure, I walked into that locker room and said to my team what normal people would label irrational, "Fellas, I don't care what that scoreboard says. We can beat that team." In other words, youthful and dumb naivete. When we returned to school, I assembled the group and showed them a calendar with the date in February when we played St. Benedict at home. I circled that date and said, "Between now and then, we are going to get better every day.

Then, we will let the chips fall where they may," or as the varsity coach, Bill Schaefer put it every gameday, "It's in the hands of the basketball gods now!"

I never brought up that game until the beginning of that February week. We prepared well: we talked about the resilience we required; we decided to put all the guts we possessed into our defense; we had to outrebound them and show the mental poise when the game was truly on the line. We beat St. Benedict that night 40-31. You read right. The team followed the game plan of patient offense, relentless defense, good shooting, and controlled tempo to the level of excellence we needed. We were masters at the free throw line. St. Benedict seasoned that recipe by getting technical fouls in the fourth quarter. At that point the players knew the game was theirs, and I knew I wanted to coach for a long time and put the dedication into the profession it deserved. This book is a compilation of that dedication.

 ## REFLECTION

TOM McCORMACK

Throughout the moments of joy and celebration and those times of sorrow and devastation, you learn to navigate the highs and the lows and know there is much to learn from both. Some say that the definition of insanity is "doing the same thing over and over again and expecting a different result." Well, when coaches and players trust in the process, the correct term is "driven."

In my first year as a head coach in 1984-85, I had the good fortune of taking over an established program. Under Stett's great leadership, it was not only used to winning, but a program where the players were ready, willing, and able to do the things necessary to compete at an extremely high level. We spent seven years on the same staff, six of those at Immaculate Conception. I had a front row seat as the program took a positive step every season. Coach Wooden's saying, "The will to win is insignificant, unless the will to work to win is greater" took on real meaning at I.C. and everywhere Stett coached and played. We won 23 games that year and made it to the sectional championship where we lost to St. Mel, the eventual state champion. Much of the coaching was player-driven from the basketball education they had received in the program.

Well, I had the road map and the directions for building a program, and in the next season (1985-86), I was given the opportunity. Talk about a challenge. Don Crandall had just become the new athletic director at Conant High School, and I was his first hire. His understanding, patience, and guidance were crucial in building the basketball program. The key word was "build," not fix, and building takes time. The remnants of any success the program had achieved had been gone for many seasons. We were starting the program from scratch and saw it as a tremendous opportunity to build something to last. Repetition and building on fundamentals were the keys that led to progress, then to winning.

We began that first season with two essential sophomores, no experienced leadership nor many positive expectations from the returning players. Neither of the sophomores was ready for varsity competition. One was a point guard and the other a post player, so at least we had a good combination to develop. We did not come close to winning a single game that first year and only won two the second year, but we saw the gap closing. The competitive spirit of those two players was an everyday drive. Their competitiveness in practices was influencing the team's personality. A defensive stopper started to develop with some role players in the second season when many of the games were closer, but we could not finish.

The leadership the two now-juniors modeled in the off-season was critical to our progress. We made our biggest jump that summer going into that third year. Now it was player-driven. They made sure the team's dedication to the summer camp, leagues, and open gyms was non-negotiable. The clear message was," Lead, follow, or get out of the way!" After that summer, winning was an expectation, not an exception. Playing hard, smart, and together had substance now.

During our third year in the last game of the conference season at Barrington High School, we won a tough game on the road. That type of victory was foreign up to that point. That four-teenth win of the season assured us of a winning record and at least one win against every team in the conference.

The two players, our inexperienced sophomores two years ear-lier, had lived through it all and had led the way. However, the real victory was in the journey the players, coaches, support staff, and families shared over three seasons. An even bigger victory was the motivation and example passed to the teams that followed. Two years later we had our first 20-win season and played in our first super-sectional. It would not be our last. The victory was in the details.

INTRODUCTION

WHILE ON A TRIP TO the American Southwest, the Swiss psychiatrist and psychoanalyst Carl Jung visited an Indian tribe and noticed that every morning a group of elders left the village before dawn for the top of a mountain to greet the sun. They believed that failure to carry out that task would lead to the sun not appearing. Jung reflected on the importance and significance that daily visit gave to their lives and their task (quoted in *Stop Whining; Start Winning* 246).

Similarly, finding meaning and purpose for your working with kids through the sport of basketball is invaluable. Meaning and purpose will sustain you through the rough times and help you enjoy the successes even more. May this book assist you for finding more meaning and value for your own relationship for coaching basketball and coaching it well.

Throughout our years working on the same staff and then heading our own programs, we have shared a similar philosophy about the ingredients for creating and sustaining a quality basketball program. We were never satisfied with having a good team here and there. Of course, good teams support an outstanding program; some can argue that without great teams, there is no program. However, it is within the concept of sustainability that great programs live. And breathe. And benefit the players down the road. Thus, we decided to document our thoughts about the traits necessary for the creation, the progress, and the consistency for a terrific program. Moreover, excellent programs can happen on many levels of talent or age groups.

We created an acronym from "P-R-O-G-R-A-M" that highlights certain traits. If you sat down with the same idea, we are confident you would decide on suitable replacements, but the following are our choices. Under each asset, we describe details for that particular quality, details for coaches to ponder and deliver to their players. These details have invigorated our own programs and have led to many victories. They are the result of a combined nine-plus decades of planning, trial-and-error, creativity, frustration, and achievement. Moreover, we believe these concepts can assist coaches who mentor any sport, any parent who works with their children, and any player who dreams big. Basketball coaches are our primary targets, but as any sports aficionado knows, sports deliver both victories on the scoreboards and in personal development.

Each section of "P-R-O-G-R-A-M" begins with thought-provoking statements by icons of the game. Discussion stems from those quotations. Some personal reflections embellish those points. We include details which provide suggestions, methods, and/or techniques for that asset. Because you can find particular sections and/or suggestions for your own improvement, you can skip around in the book to your preferences, but with an initial reading, we suggest you read the book as it is laid out.

No matter the level you coach or your individual responsibilities at that level, we believe these concepts will make you think and more importantly, help you improve your approach to your players, to other coaches, to parents, to the community, and to yourself. Enjoy your morning coffee, mid-afternoon, and/or bedtime reading and thinking.

~Tom Anstett and Tom McCormack

LETTER TO COACHES

Dear Coaches and Readers,

Thank you for selecting our book. The structure of this book is such that you can skip to whatever section or concept within a section you feel needs your attention and study. Before you dive into the material, please complete the following self-evaluation by writing down your responses with as much detail as possible. Through your responses, you are able to concentrate on areas for self-growth. There is a plethora of detail in each section; we know you will find plenty of insights, no matter where you see yourself as a coach now.

1. What is the important groundwork to lay for building a lasting program?

2. How do you model resilience for everyone in your program?

3. Identify your philosophy and emphases for the off-season.

4. Toughness in basketball can have many meanings; how do you define it?

5. We all talk about the importance of rebounding. How much do you really emphasize it?

6. Does the level of attention from your players and coaching staff lead to the execution you desire? Give examples.

7. As a coach are you aiming to be adequate or to master the game? What steps are you taking now to achieve that goal?

P – PREPARATION

GOOD DAY!

Pull up a comfortable chair. Select a cold beverage of your choice. This section contains pertinent information concerning a factor every coach determines—preparation. If your amount of preparation comes anything close to what each of our wonderful wives possesses, you will relish the details and suggestions we offer in this chapter. We are begging the question for offering reasons why preparation is so essential, but those "compelling whys" remain part of a successful foundation for the enduring success of a basketball program. Coaches need good players; that is a given. Yet, when presented with good players, good coaches' preparation becomes paramount to any eventual success. Coaches cannot just roll the balls out when they have battle-tested and quality players in an upcoming season. Conversely, if the talent is below par and players need more development, preparation is just as vital. Maybe keep in mind the words of an old farmer as you prepare for a season or as you progress through a season, "Every path has a few puddles."

THE COMPELLING WHYS

- PREPARATION buys credibility for the coach in the eyes of his/her players.
- PREPARATION is a first step and a foundation toward building confidence within the coach and the players.
- PREPARATION requires coaches to seek more knowledge for having a sense of the game's changes.
- PREPARATION keeps everyone in the program improving during a rough season.
- PREPARATION comes in two facets: developing players and developing teams.
- PREPARATION is a good example for motivating players, no matter the time of the season.
- PREPARATION lessens, even eliminates, excuses.

A LIST OF THE PARTS IN THIS CHAPTER:

Team Preparation—
Points to Ponder and The Big Three within a BIG TEN

Individual Preparation—
Skill sets, defining roles, guarding the ball, talking at both ends, attitude

Five More Preparation Points

Practice—
Prime points, checklist, models, sample plans

Flow Charts—
Skills evaluation for each year

Season Breakdown—
Early-season, mid-season, late-season

Offense philosophy

Games—
Game prep, game management, post-game

POINTS TO PONDER

 REFLECTION

TOM McCORMACK

In my first year at Conant High School in 1985-86, we were awful (0-24) and lost by an average of 16.7 points per game (ppg). In the second year we only won two games, but the average "improved" to losing by 6.7 points ppg. We did a much better job with things like quality possessions, shot selection, post touches, box outs, charges, loose balls, and acceptance of roles. Our victories were in the things we could control and the things we tweaked each year. Free throws, rebounding, and turnovers became our constant non-negotiables. Over the years, well-executed possessions with quality assisted shots and limiting the opponent to one contested shot or a turnover became the two biggest factors for evaluating our progress. These constant goals resulted in 13 twenty-win seasons, five conference titles, seven division titles, 14 regional championships, four sectional titles, and two appearances in the state finals over my 32 years as head coach at that school. Beyond and because of the pursuit of excellence, the victories were in each journey within each season.

Preparation contains various forms of thought and evaluation for both the team and the individual. Let's take a look at each factor.

TEAM

One of the first priorities for sustaining any progress is a unified and competent staff. Over the years, we have been fortunate to work with some excellent assistant coaches. Sometimes, hiring decisions can be the luck of the draw. At times, head coaches are in the position of inheriting rather than choosing their assistants. Occasionally, those coaches do not have basketball as a high priority, nor might they be proficient teachers. Head coaches have to be dutiful and diligent in this area. They must be able to "teach the teachers" in the necessary skills and philosophy. After all, it is the head coach's head on the line. Especially important is the freshman coach. Beginning those players with proper instruction in the fundamentals and the system the head coach deems valid are crucial to the program's lifeline. Moreover, head coaches can help the assistants develop confidence by giving them responsibility. There is a more complete breakdown later in this chapter regarding the management of staff.

Three essential measurements for team progress: 1) Execution, regardless of outcome; 2) Improvement, regardless of outcome; 3) Intensity and communication (harder to measure).

1. EXECUTION, REGARDLESS OF OUTCOME, relies on a good system that fits the talent and the proper use of fundamentals to establish the continuity for that system. Coaches need to be able to break down the components for players in practices for successful application in games. Does "regardless of outcome" imply that we don't care about the final score? Hardly. Helping players establish team goals for the season, the month, and/or a particular opponent can assist players to find reliability and improvement in their weekly performances.

2. IMPROVEMENT, REGARDLESS OF OUTCOME. Losing by less margins? Winning by greater margins? Beating a certain opponent in the second round of conference after a colossal loss the first time? Each one can be a sign of improvement for a team. The key point here is that each game needs the proper preparation and evaluation. Not enough time is spent on evaluating a team's performance. Moreover, emphasizing winning over improvement, especially at pre-college levels, distorts players' thinking about individual progress. Players and coaches do play to win; it is the pre-game and post-game that require good planning and precise follow-up. One might think of those phases in these terms: the pre-game is the mental and physical preparation, i.e. the "homework." The game is the actual exam. The post-game is the grade for the exam and the plan for improvement. Very similar stages to the classroom experience.

3. INTENSITY AND COMMUNICATION are harder to measure. Players believe they are playing hard. Often, a discrepancy exists between what players believe and what the coach believes about the level of competitiveness players are revealing. Coaches have to be great salesmen here; they must convince their charges that the coaches measure intensity and communication. In addition, watching game video never lies. Showing the players their plusses and limitations enhances trust and the coach's credibility.

INDIVIDUAL

Over the course of time, we have heard the same thing from players and parents, "You're destroying my (child's) confidence." True confidence emerges from the success that happens when preparation and opportunity intersect. Preparation is the part where a lot of coaches and players fall short. Confidence and preparation go hand in hand. Confidence is meaningless without good preparation. Shakespeare's All's Well That Ends Well, although used in a different context, today means that as long as the end is met, it really doesn't matter the means for accomplishing that end. We call this outlook "fool's gold." Our point is that a player might have a good result once in a while, but if it comes from something a player or team has really not worked on, eventually the same action will let a team down. For example, a mediocre player makes an ill-advised 3-point shot. A lucky make can actually do more harm than good to a player's and a team's decision making and execution down the road. In individual games, free throws, rebounds, and turnovers are our chief statistical factors, but these pieces can vary based on the makeup that year. Here are two important questions to begin total preparation, especially for high school coaches who can't recruit specific types of talent:

Do the players have to fit into the system,
or does the system have to fit the players?

What are the non-negotiables?

The answers to those questions need to be crystal clear to all assistant coaches and players. Also, administrators and parents should be aware of every expectation.

Trends of today may influence but should not dictate what we emphasize. Certainly, we attend clinics and college practices, watch training videos, etc., to keep learning. Because of the nature of the high school game and the types of players available, some of the "old school stuff," like the mid-range jump shot and back-to-the-basket post play might best suit the talent level in a particular season. For a few players, those skills will be mastered. Remember, most coaches have to work with who walks in the door.

REFLECTION

TOM ANSTETT

I took over three different programs, each was coming off a series of poor seasons. Regardless of the talent level, I first tried to build progress and evaluate it at the defensive end. I knew we needed more time to create a sound offense and to find and develop at least three scorers every year. Defense, however, can be taught and emphasized from day one as a source of pride for any team and can be measured with some important statistics (charges, blocks, deflections, block outs, loose balls, scores off defensive stops, consecutive stops, etc.) Many coaches teach defense; too many do not emphasize it every day. I feel that if a team defends poorly in its half-court defense, there is no team. Period.

Individual Progress

The following are suggestions for players' individual improvement during the season. The 3-point line and the shot clock have had an enormous impact on the skill development and direction of the game. Today the term "position-less player" refers to players with good ballhandling skill, 3-point shooting efficiency, and the talent to play and guard multiple positions. Decision making is another valued commodity because at its core, basketball remains a cerebral game.

Whether or not the shot clock is in effect, it is extremely important to design an offense based on acute floor spacing around the skills of the available players. In the high school game, most coaches use role players with limited, multi-dimensional skills. Once again, the system must enhance players' abilities. We encouraged players that the time to experiment is during their work on their individual games in the off-season or at practice. Never in a game. For example, we did not allow players to attempt dunks in a game unless they had dunked at least three times in a row at practice in a full scrimmage. Similarly, unless players demonstrated they can make eight 3s in a minute or less without a rebounder, they were not shooting 3s. It's not that we wanted to discourage these types of plays. Quite the contrary. We removed the guess work and sent the message: If you want to do it, that's great. Work on it in the offseason, so that in a game situation, it's a natural reaction and not a thought process. Once players had repeated the efficiency and acquired the confidence for performance of a particular skill at practice, then in the appropriate situation, they had the green light, regardless of the result.

Defining the appropriate situation is what team and scrimmage time at practice should make evident. Players who improve their individual skills will also enhance programs that use a shot clock. Teams will not always be able to lean on the best shooter or player at end-of-the-clock situations. With the shot clock, more players will be in situations where they have to make a play and cannot get the ball to the "go-to" player or to the creative point guard. This development accentuates the importance of individual progress on the "Big 3." That progress promotes good basketball within the parameters of a shot clock.

THE BASKETBALL

Once the team is selected, the players receive various items of equipment: practice and game uniforms, warmup gear, water bottles, and so forth. Many programs keep the basketballs on a rack that is locked away, rolled out before practice, and locked away after practice. We issued all players in the program their own basketball to be responsible for during the season. Storing it and bringing it to practice every day was each player's responsibility. Varsity players got new basketballs and the lower levels received the previous season's basketballs. The rule was if you lost it, you bought it. We lost very few. We wanted all players in the program to have access to a ball anytime they wanted. It is the most important piece of equipment for skill work in the game, just like the soldier who gets his/her rifle at boot camp. Players were responsible to take diligent care of it and master its many uses.

Basketballs are not cheap, and we always ordered the same ones used in our state tournament. Nice uniforms, shoes, and all the other gear are cool to wear and look good but to really be good, the players needed to put the time in with the ball. Basketballs were always priority number one in our budget or in any fundraising plan each season.

TRIPLE THREAT POSITION

Before we go into individual fundamentals and their teaching progressions, we want to establish the rock principle for all of our players to understand and execute. We believe that the triple threat position is the primary fundamental that players need to establish in their individual games to read the defense properly and make the best team decision that their skill sets will allow. Simply put, triple threat means players' facing the basket with the readiness to shoot, pass, or dribble the ball. All players-post, perimeter, shooters, scorers, non-shooters or scorers, role players-need to apply and master this essential fundamental. Too often we see players catch the ball and immediately dribble or turn their backs to the defenders. Sometimes this action is a read

before the catch or taught as in the Dribble Drive Offense. What we are trying to accomplish is to establish a firm habit of reading the defense and making the proper decision.

The teaching concepts are:

- Basic triple threat position is shooting hand side foot slightly in front of pivot foot, knees slightly and comfortably bent, ball in shot-ready shooting pocket position, and eyes on the rim

- The pivot and jab step with the foot opposite the shooting hand almost always being the pivot foot

- Apply the 5 principles of balance (p. 32), crucial to explosiveness

- Hand position on the ball is always in the shot ready position

- Short and long jab steps both on-side and crossover. On-side being the jab foot, shooting hand side, and crossover being the pivot foot, non-shooting hand side

- Rocker step, backstep on the shooting hand side and opposite the pivot foot

- Shot/shot fake or pass/pass fake on short jab steps. On all other steps, the ball goes securely to the hip of the fake side
- Bring the ball to the shooting pocket on all steps back into triple threat position
- Eyes stay pointed to the rim to help maintain vision and balance

If they are closely guarded, players need to understand that on the catch, they have a total of 12 seconds with the ball to avoid a 5-second turnover. Four seconds before they must dribble, shoot, or pass; four more seconds after they pick up the dribble; and four more seconds before they must dribble, shoot, or pass. Establishing the habit of a good triple threat makes players more comfortable playing cat and mouse with their defender. Players become more efficient one on one and team players. It makes slower players quicker and quick players even harder to contest and contain. We are not advocating a player actually take that much time, holding the ball. Some coaches believe today that triple threat position actually slows the game too much. This fundamental position on the catch should actually aid the quickness of a decision or action when done efficiently. As good as he was in all areas, Michael Jordan was a terrific triple threat player, especially during his last three championship seasons with the Bulls. We suggest viewing YouTube or any video of him during that period for a look at an expert master of triple threat position.

Triple threat position is the starting and finishing point of the Big 3.

THE BIG 3 IN A BIG TEN

BALLHANDLING, SHOOTING, and PASSING—the skills that continually evolve, but remain the backbone of the evaluation of players, regardless of their natural gifts.

> "A good basketball player does three skills well:
> shooting, dribbling, and passing.
> Why not work on those three things?"
>
> ~Pete Carril
> Former Princeton University Coach

1. Ballhandling

Ballhandling, the primary skill involved in scoring today, ranks arguably higher than proper shooting mechanics. Basic skills like speed dribble, protective dribble, back up dribble, offhand development, change of pace dribble, and pull back-crossover are only the starting points for the better players. Creative ballhandling is almost a must for scorers. A couple other examples of these skills today are the dribble drive into a 1-2- jump stop, the "Euro Step," and the step-back jump shot. All are taught and used today, especially at more advanced levels.

Ballhandling skills, whether for role players or advanced players, is an example of the way coaches make decisions about personnel and development of players. Who is allowed to dribble against a press? For whom does a coach run an isolation or ball screen play at the end of a game, a quarter, or a clock situation? Is the point guard knowledgeable about who should get the ball in those situations? These decisions, among others, all involve various levels of preparation.

We practiced ballhandling daily; however, players improve this skill primarily in the off-season. During sprints in conditioning lines at practice, players dribbled a basketball or two basketballs. Ballhandling was always a part of warm-up and a point communicated when necessary during every drill or scrimmage.

Most high school teams do not have an abundance of position-less players; therefore, we included in the off-season section the list of ballhandling skills and drills for 1, 2, and 3 sport athletes. These include workouts for the athletes who are primarily basketball players and for those who are not. We certainly wanted to develop as many multi-dimensional players as possible. On the other hand, most teams are fortunate to have a couple of "go to" players or prolific scorers in the same season. Three of them on the floor at a time is a lot for most high school teams, and those teams that have that luxury are hard to guard and usually have great seasons.

To repeat, in today's game, the ability to handle the basketball with a high skill level is a crucial skill. Coaches need to ponder the question of how well they are implementing and teaching this skill within their practice preparations.

We have all the off-season drills (basic and advanced) listed in the Off-season section in this book.

2. Shooting

Would you rather be lucky or good? Danny Ainge, the current general manager of the Boston Celtics remarked on his preparation for his NBA seasons that he had to make 15,000 shots in the summer. That's 15,000 makes. The correct answer? Good. Luck follows.

With all due respect to Shakespeare, coaches cannot accept the "all's well that ends well" proposition, or the "Hey, coach, it went in, didn't it?" A win or a successful result to a play might mask a lack of skill or good judgement. This approach is particularly true in shooting and is why using film is so important for shooting mechanics. It is easier to start from scratch than to correct a faulty habit repeated over time. True confidence comes from the many correct repetitions that lead to shooting mastery. Once preparation has planted firm roots, it is usually a matter of time for opportunity to appear for both coaches and players. We told players, "When opportunity knocks, you better be home. It will surely knock once, but rarely knocks again unless you answer the first time." This doesn't mean a player has to make every shot. Players-shooters actually hurt the team if they don't take the shot. If they have invested the time properly, they are less fretful from the self-imposed pressure of having to make everything. It becomes much easier to deal with outcomes and move to what's next.

It is desirable for a shooter/scorer to possess a 2-guard mentality. That mental approach covers any position, one not bothered by a miss or consecutive misses. That player is always ready to shoot again. That mentality is not for everyone, just as leadership is not. On Coach Paul Westhead's great Loyola Marymount teams, Jeff Fryer might have had the best job ever for a 2-guard. He ran to the right corner and shot a three with every touch if possible, no matter the situation. The clutch scorers need to have a very short memory for failure. The best scorers will miss a few in a row; they also think that they have a few coming. They are 50% shooters and they shoot above that percentage in every workout they complete. Those scorers do not leave the gym until 50% is achieved.

Players who experience the confidence born through opportunity and success from correct repetition and relentless training are never satisfied with proficiency. Mastery must be the goal for the prolific shooter. Coaches need to challenge their scorers and set the bar a little higher each time their players reach a goal. Truly dedicated players will do this on their own. Most players who picture themselves as great scorers do not complete that vision with the needed dedication; many need to learn ways to keep challenging themselves. The thoroughbreds, those who master shooting, belong in Level 4 of preparation. We describe these levels after the off-season section in this book.

Most players like to shoot, so even though shooting skills are not easy to master, getting players to work on them is easier than less glamorous skills. Frustration becomes reality if bad mechanics are present. We worked with many players at shooting clinics and with individuals on proper shooting mechanics. With players whose poor mechanics needed improvement, we took making shots out of the process in the early stages. Their shot needed to be built from the ground up. We had players shoot without a ball, so their focus was the actual technique from start to finish. Seeing the ball go through the hoop is the ultimate goal, one for constant visualization. We told players they could expect to get worse before they improved. First, we demonstrated what a good shot and shooting mechanics looked like. We broke down every phase from the footwork all the way to the follow through, with all the points in between. One suggestion is the "B-E-E-F" method. Balance starting with legs, core, and chin-Eyes focusing on one part of the rim-Elbow tucked in on a slant-Follow through-reaching up and over with arm straight after release and fingers spread. B.E.E.F. begins without a ball and in front of the rim. Gradually, the shooter adds the ball and moves out a couple of steps at a time. This shot is one-handed; the guide (off) hand is not part of this technique until later. Filming the shooter from different angles is a fine tool to use. Shooting a ball back and forth to a partner with the partners critiquing each other is another good drill.

Coach John Wooden said, "Good players can perform the fundamental skills quickly." When working on building any fundamental or advanced skill, thinking about the process, visualizing it, and then evaluating it are key parts of the process. The ultimate goal is to get to the point where the shot becomes a natural action. Executing and precisely repeating the correct action in competitive drills and game situations happen because of the study, thought, and repetition that has occurred building the skill. In a game the jump shot needs to be a habit of correct action, not a thought process.

Of the various types of shots, layups and various types of finishes off the dribble at the rim, floaters in the lane, the mid-range pull up jump shot, back to the basket moves, the rhythm 3, the step-back 3, and the free throw are only a few for practice. Through constant application of technique, game speed repetition, imagination, and efficient use of time, many players can develop into fine shooters and master one or two particular moves they are comfortable using at any time in a game. On the other hand, just like some people might try to be bridge builders but do not have the tools to accomplish that skill, not all players develop into scorers. That basketball level takes precise acumen and a toughness not all players relish or possess. By senior year, the cream has risen to the top in terms of identifying scorers, not just shooters. Proper shooting mechanics, volume of repetition, and ultimate confidence are the ingredients for making a great shooter. A great scorer needs ballhandling skills with a dominant mentality. Whether in the post or on the perimeter, every great scorer should possess a signature move and an efficient counter to that move. We have more shooting explanation, shooting drills, and skill work in the Off-season section.

3. Passing and Receiving

MAXIM #1:

"Never try to teach a pig to sing."
*Translation: A mediocre passer should learn to be proficient
at handing the ball off.*

MAXIM #2:

*One of the best non-definitions of a great passer:
"Well, I can't really define what one is,
but ask a coach who doesn't have one."*

MAXIM #3:

*"The pass is a very powerful team builder; whereas the dribble
(unless by the coach's design) can destroy the spirit of teams
and crack the foundation of team play."*

~Kevin Eastman
Ex-NBA Assistant Coach

Passing

Is passing a lost art? If the answer is yes, then why don't coaches concentrate on polishing this facet of the Big 3 since passing remains one of the most important fundamentals to any good offense? After all, if a coach has players who can score, isn't precise passing an essential to get them the ball? Passing is not as glamorous as shooting or ballhandling, but without it, players belong in a tier below the category of the complete player. Complete players not only possess the technical skills involved in the Big 3 but also the appropriate application of those skills in game situations. As passers, they know where the ball should go, how to get it there, and when to get it there. The basic fundamentals of passing are easier to learn than ballhandling and shooting. The real mastery of passing is in the decision of which type of pass to make and when to make it. Passing in a game is like playing chess, except all the pieces might be moving at the same time. Great passing is usually associated with point guards but can come from any position including post players. A great passer will lead a teammate into a move or shot, sometimes with the pass receiver not even realizing it. Just like great scorers and ballhandlers, a team's offensive system should be built around getting a high volume of touches for its best passers or decision makers. Once players learn and establish the specific fundamentals, they should practice passing in 3-on-3 half-court and full court (both with and without dribbling), then 4-on-4, and eventually 5-on-5. This skill cannot be underestimated or overlooked.

Want more concrete evidence as to the importance of passing? In the article *Does Team Chemistry Actually Exist?*, author Jamey Austin discusses the Golden State Warriors when Steve Kerr took over as head coach in 2014. Kerr inherited a talented, but underperforming team. Meeting with Sammy Gelfand, the team's metrics coach, Kerr wanted to figure out how to improve the team with the assistance of analytics. Kerr wanted a more ball movement-offense with extra passes like he used from his playing days, but he needed hard evidence. Gelfand found that evidence. The previous season, the Warriors had averaged just 247 passes per game, by far the worst in the NBA. But he also found that when the team passed the ball more than three times per possession, it led the league in points per possession. The magic number was 300. The 300 passes per game benchmark combined sophisticated analysis with core basketball teamwork fundamentals, what Ryan describes as "a tribal reliance on one another." It was brilliant. Gelfand had figured out that 300 passes would mean more points, plus "an increase in passing not only would unite players around a specific goal, but it would also solidify a team-first mindset by constantly sharing the ball," writes Ryan. The Warriors won the NBA championship that year, their first in 40 years, and averaged 315.9 passes per game. They were arguably one of the most exciting teams to watch in NBA history, largely due to their style of play which, with such an emphasis on sharing the ball, showcased visible joy, unselfishness, and camaraderie. (Ladders in Apple News, quoted from *Intangibles* by Joan Ryan)

Coaches, perhaps a good experiment for one season is to measure the passing analytic for your team by comparing the number of passes in wins vs. losses. In any case, good passing teams pass up opponents.

PASSING "DOs"

For Coaches' Teaching Points within Players' Levels of Ability

DO learn, coaches, the "passing IQ" of each of your players. On any team, players possess various levels of passing IQ. The assist or the simple pass that leads to the next pass or the one that keeps the possession a live threat is a mix of players' basic and IQ skills. In high school the only time that a pass should be forced is if it's a clock situation.

DO teach the techniques for these basic passes: chest pass, bounce pass, skip pass, lob pass, baseball pass, two-handed overhead, and handoff in both full and half-court drills. These are not hard to master, even for role players with limited skill. A simple drill to employ is to line up two players (1 and 3) behind one sideline and two players (2 and 4) behind the opposite sideline. One ball starts the drill. Player 1 throws a baseball pass to player 2; player 1 follows that pass, lands in a two-foot jump stop, and receives a chest pass from player 2. Player 2 follows the pass and receives a handoff in a reverse pivot from player 1. Player 1 sprints behind player 4 on the sideline. Player 2 throws a bounce pass to player 3. The drill continues from the start. Players must call the name of the receiver to whom they pass, and each team yelled the number of consecutive passes. This drill keeps the players hustling yet commits players to executing accurate passes. The drill can be competitive: The coach can start each group with the goal of the first group of four to complete 25 passes. However, if the ball ever hit the floor (excluding the bounce pass), that team went back to zero. Such fun!

Coaches with Players with a Higher Passing IQ

DO teach advanced passing skills such as behind the back, between the legs, lob to the rim, and the look-off or away. The good players use those particular passes as a change of direction, a ball reversal option, or a penetration to score or create. Some passes need to be thrown with extra or less back spin, top spin, or velocity. The development of touch, placement, and timing are higher IQ passing skills. Having a practical use, these passes are not for show. That being said, practice is the time to experiment, not during a game.

DO teach the easy pass: Passes that are deflected or lost result in basketball-death. If a team shoots around 50%, that's about one point per possession that each turnover costs a team. A team averaging around 12 turnovers a game is a good average, but that total also amounts to 12 ppg for the opponent. Any more than that total is very difficult to survive, especially in a close game. If the team shooting percentage is lower, that ratio is even more costly. Players need to understand that when it comes to degree of difficulty, they need to stay within their range of passing skill.

DO see the defensive help: The passer must be able to see the defense behind the intended target, so the receiver is not led into a charge, a travel, or a double team. This is where a pass fake or eye (look-off) fake can be effective, especially when trying to get the ball to a key player. The passer needs to read if the intended target has beaten both the defender and the help. This skill is true against any defense, man, zone, box and 1, etc.

DO be a threat to score in order to be a threat to pass. Making the defender guard by being in triple threat position or by penetrating with the ball first forces the defense toward the ball and away from the pass receiver. The action that precedes the pass (pass fake, eye fake, dribble penetration, back up dribble, etc.) is as important as the pass itself. "Fake a pass to make a pass."

DO understand that half the shot is in the accurate pass. A good pass made with the intention of creating a shot is a confidence builder for both passer and shooter.

DO know the seven passing lanes: the top of the head, the two ears, each waist area, and the two knees.

DO pass away from defense, not to your teammate.

DO point out and applaud the assist, multiple efforts, hustle plays, etc.

Against Trapping Teams

DO work on strong pivots, both a pull-back and a split move dribble, avoid corners and sidelines, and practice eye progression of strong, middle, diagonal, and reverse vs. presses.

DO learn to fake high-pass low and to fake low-pass high. These vertical fakes require a medium stance with good ball grip, pivoting on balance, and reading the defender. Those fakes are effective after a dribble has been used. Low means ankle; high means by either ear or over the head of the defender.

PASSING DON'Ts

For Teaching Points and Player Development

DON'T leave the feet to pass. The majority of the time the result is a turnover. Quite simply, this action is a bad habit.

DON'T make one-hand passes; they cannot be pulled back.

DON'T throw to a voice because accuracy suffers. The alert defensive player loves it though.

DON'T attempt passes having a high degree of difficulty, the "Spectacular Pass Syndrome." Unlike gymnastics and diving, no extra points are awarded for degree of difficulty.

DON'T throw certain passes to players who can't catch them. Experience and familiarity with teammates will lead to better verbal and visual communication. Both will enhance "the play before the play."

SITUATION PASSING

For Coaches to Notice and Teach Correct Passing Decisions

With most passing drills or situations, players call names of receivers.

- Fast breaks and transition start with a strong outlet pass.
- Press attack: Two-foot jump stops, pivots, and pass fakes are very effective weapons vs. presses, pressure, and traps.
- Inbounds pass vs. presses
- Half-court offense and special plays
- Inbound plays from both baseline and sideline
- End of clock situations and plays

Passing On the Perimeter

Practice chest and skip passes on the perimeter instead of bounce passes. Perimeter passes intercepted turn into transition points by the defense. Time to substitute?

Passing Off a Screen to a Cutter or a Screener

Reading whether the cutter or the screener is the one who will be open is key here. A nice drill has two pairs of players and two basketballs. One pair will execute a screening situation, and the other pair will pass a basketball to each for a shot. The player opening on the arc will receive a chest or skip pass, and the basket cutter will receive a bounce or lob pass. They will each shoot and retrieve their own rebound, then switch roles with the other or next pair.

Passing Off Dribble Penetration

This is an advanced skill. Unlike the one-two stop preferred for shooting, the two-foot jump stop is the most reliable for passing. It brings the driver/passer into much better body control, allowing for a pivot in either direction and a better decision. The pass may be a bounce pass, a lob pass into the post, or a kick-out pass to a perimeter player. The two-foot jump stop also allows for a good shot or pass fake to freeze the defense.

Passing To a Posted Player

A simple pass in terms of basic skill but more complicated in terms of decision making. Touch, placement, timing, and faking with both the ball and eyes come into play. First, we did not pass into the post unless the posted player demanded the ball and posted up with authority. The passer saw the uniform number of the posted player. Second, with the ball on the wing, players practice passing into the post from triple threat position on the wing to keep the player guarding the ball from sagging. Fake hi and bounce pass low or fake low and air pass high are two effective setups for this entry pass. Lob passes occur if the post was dead fronted with no weakside help and only to the baseline side, not the middle. The passer aims for the corner of the backboard and the outside arm of the receiver. Holding the position and seal, the receiver does not go for the pass until the ball is over his/her head. Whenever possible, a good shooter should position on the wing of the designated post player.

To supplement passing into the low post, establishment of a ball side triangle is critical. On the post-up on the ball side, there should be an option to pass the ball into the post from both the wing or the top, with a player positioned in each area. On the back side, two players space, one high and one wide outside the arc, to keep the post player isolated. This makes help and double teaming in the post difficult for the defense. Spacing on offense is always important when establishing a low post presence.

If the opponent fronts the post, a pivot and seal move by the post player with good spacing on the weak side makes a post entry pass from the top difficult to defend.

Any time the ball is passed into the post, a coordination of movement and spacing is necessary for both wings and the top.

Whenever a player catches the ball in the low post and is only guarded by one player, the first option is score. As soon as there is more than one defender guarding the ball in the low post, perimeter players need to be spaced so that it is impossible for any defender on the perimeter to guard two people simultaneously.

Pivoting, pass faking, and limited dribbling-one dribble preferable-by the post player can slow down any help or double team action by the defense. One maxim for low post play is: The closer to the basket, the slower the play.

Outlet Passing

Probably the best tutorial available on the outlet pass is video of the late Wes Unseld. His outlet passes were a lethal offensive weapon that turned defense into offense and put points on the board-all in the blink of an eye. There are various systems of outlet pass and fast break designs. Some prefer an outlet pass release to the sideline or middle, and some just have the point guard get the ball. We taught the receiver of the outlet pass to show two hands high, call out and establish position at the top of the key extended close to the sideline with his/her back to the sideline for better court vision, and then take a step to the ball to receive the pass. Upon receiving the outlet pass we wanted the ball: 1. Passed ahead deep if possible, and 2. Driven with three dribbles or fewer to the offensive top of the key. Then, it becomes a decision to use the brake or the gas pedal. The stutter step by the driver is an efficient fundamental to use at that spot to make the defender commit one way or the other.

Receiving

Although receiving is passing's blood brother, this fundamental gets even less attention and instruction than its partner. They are complementary; one without the other does not achieve much, other than turnovers and off-balance decisions. Passes are caught with the eyes on the ball into the hands. Proper receiving of passes should be an emphasis in summer camps and early in the regular season.

Receiving Techniques:

- Get free by a crossover seal to "L" move (or) back step from defender, so when the defender turns to look, the offensive player sprints out to position for reception.
- Call "ball."

- Give target with the outside hand.

- Aggressively come to ball with a jump stop. Even better is a jump behind the pass so that pivoting is not necessary. That jump takes practice, and the passer passes to the inside at the shooting pocket.

- Eyes: See the ball into the hands and catch with a block and tuck. Early in the season have all players over-exaggerate the follow through on every pass and look into the tuck.

- Pivot to triple threat.

Receiving Against Traps:

- Make strong two-foot jump stops on the catch to enable a pivot in any direction.

- Come back to meet the pass.

- Outfight any defender for the ball.

- Keep a pressure release in the middle of the floor.

- When in the middle with the ball, pivot and see the floor ahead before passing or dribbling to avoid a charge, travel, or bad pass. Someone will be coming from behind. Stay wide and strong just like in the post.

- With proper spacing, it will be difficult for one defender to cover two people.

4. Setting and Receiving Screens

Screens? Picks? What are those? Who needs them, anyway? In the present basketball world and in the offenses taught worldwide, the emphasis has become more of entertaining, freewheeling movements, with fundamentals suffering. We can count on one hand the number of precise, body-contact screens during a game. With so much concentration on perimeter players' dribbling and penetration skills, good screens have become analogous to the extinction of the two-hand, underhanded free throw or the loss of the jock strap. Moreover, in the majority of occasions where a screen with good contact and an opening to the ball or a roll to the hoop occurs, good results for that offense happens, with either a basket or a foul on the defense. Those results are not coincidental.

Therefore, our purpose here is to reacquaint coaches with the dynamics of relevant and physical screens, both on and off the ball. Slips or brush screens have their places since they are typically read by the offensive player as to what the defense is allowing. We are discussing a set play or movement within a motion or continuity offense where good screens must be a fundamental of execution. What are the key concepts of accepting and setting good screens?

**KEY: With the knowledge that a screener is the most open player on the court for a couple of seconds on almost every type of screen, the screener must open to the ball for a potential pass and scoring opportunity.

KEY POINTS FOR SETTING SCREENS ON THE BALL

- A screener has to be willing to accept contact.

- Setting screens is an unselfish, winning part of a basketball offense.

- A screener must sprint to the correct spot and angle for the setting of the screen. Once at the right spot, the screener must avoid moving.

- Screeners need a wide base at medium center with the feet wider than the shoulders and hands protecting the lower region, similar to taking a charge. Screeners aim for contact in the middle of their chests from the defender being screened. Having a wide base fulfills a basic principle of good offense: taking up court space.

- To quote one of basketball's superior teachers, the late Rick Majerus, "The key vocal is 'Wait' for the dribbler to know the screen is coming." The screener yells, "Wait." Some coaches might argue for the screener to be silent so as to avoid alerting the defense. However, there is merit to talking the game on offense, not just on defense. Better communication ensues. For example, waiting for screens with enough patience can help the screener avoid an offensive foul; if the dribbler moves too quickly and the screener is not set, blocking fouls occur, a costly turnover. In addition, we had players show a fist if their intention was to screen. With that visual signal, the player with the ball knew not to pass to a teammate coming to set a screen. Screeners role on contact with legs in a slide, similar to a defensive slide. With that slide the screener is in good balance if receiving the pass from the dribbler. An exception to the slide is the slip screen which should be a sprint and the show of a hand for either a bounce or a lob pass. A recurring error is the recipient of the screen makes a move too soon before the screener has a chance to set the screen. Once again, "Wait"—yelled three times—has to become an essential verbal command.

KEY POINTS FOR SETTING SCREENS OFF THE BALL

- Screeners need a wide base with their feet wider than the shoulders and hands protecting the lower region, again similar to taking a charge. Female basketball players set screens with their arms folded across their chests. Wide use of the legs and bent knees help to avoid serious injury to the thighs or groin. Screeners aim for contact in the middle of their chests from the defender being screened. Having a wide base takes up court space.

- Meet the defender to screen. Avoid sliding left or right. "Headhunt" the defender to be screened. Hunt for that player. Do not depend on the teammate receiving the screen to do all the work.

- Setting a backscreen or flair requires giving a step to the player being screened. The defender cannot see the screener, so one step is necessary. Conversely, for a downscreen or a post screen, when the defender can see the screener, the screener can get as close as possible. A block-to-block screen requires the screener to turn and look before moving. With that vision, the screener can find the position of the player to be screened.

- Flair screens are more guess work. These screens can result in slip and brush screens. However, some contact is always the goal.

- Once again, immediately after screening, that player opens to the ball for a potential pass and scoring opportunity. That move is a must for players to execute.

KEY POINTS FOR ACCEPTING BALL SCREENS AS THE BALLHANDLER

- Save the dribble. Players are all too anxious to put the ball on the floor. This action is a two-edged sword. It might be part of the quick offenses used today, such as the dribble-drive, but it limits the potential for beating the defender in a 1-on-1 situation. Anxious dribbling also stalls movement off the ball as players tend to watch one teammate try to create a score. Save the dribble. Give time for the screener to establish position. A possible visual in this situation is waiting for the two-foot jump stop (Hear the "stomp!") from the screener. The verbal signal is "Wait."

- Use the jab step to set up the dribble. At times, the pull-back dribble can assist setup.

- The disposition of the ballhandler is to score when receiving a ball screen. With that focus the dribbler will have good passing options if a scoring opportunity does not present itself.

- Hubie Brown, "The dribbler should take at least two dribbles away from his ball screen, especially if his defender tries to fight over the top of the screen." This action pushes the defense to make more decisions and provides proper spacing between the dribbler and the roll. In addition, this action helps the offense take up more court space. However, that maxim by Coach Brown is not a steadfast rule. Reacting to the defender is always at the heart of a good offensive move. If the defender of the dribbler goes under the screen, a step-back shot is an option off a pull-back dribble. There are numerous ways to defend ball screens. No matter how the defender reacts, the first option for the ballhandler is to create a scoring opportunity. Rick Majerus said, "A player is not a threat to pass until he is a threat to score."

- A good visual for this movement is for the player with the ball to head tap. This visual communicates the player's desire to receive a screen.

KEY POINTS FOR ACCEPTING SCREENS OFF THE BALL

- Read the defender's body and head position. Do not look at the ball too much. Reading those positions helps the offensive player receiving the screen to make the correct cut: Does he/she direct cut? Flair? Go under the screen or over? Lots of quality 3-on-3 promotes this skill. Reading the defense is the heart of quality offense.

- "Hip-to-hip." A cutter off a screen should make every attempt to run off the hip of the screener, even a slight bump is acceptable. In that way, the defender has no room to stay with the cutter. Hubie Brown, "The recipient of a screen can put his basket side hand on the hip of the screener. This technique has him coming hip-to-hip and if the cutter feels the defender coming ball side and hard, he feels it and backcuts."

- On flair screens, create distance from the screen after pushing the teammate who is setting the flair screen into the defense.

- Whatever the cut, a decisive one is in order. A hard cut is as effective as a good screen. Any cut is a hard one.

- Typically, a change of pace by the player receiving the screen is the most effective. Slow to set up, hard on the cut. Getting the defender to relax or stand up out of a defensive stance is ideal.

KEY POINTS FOR THE DRIBBLE HANDOFF

There are two types of dribble handoffs: speed or power. The dribble handoff, popular in offenses today, has made a comeback from the days of the Celtic weave. The technique is distinctly different from the ball screen. Instead of waiting for a stop, both players sprint toward one another with the receiver going behind the dribbler. Some coaches allow just a flip of the ball from passer to receiver. We taught a very specific handoff technique to avoid a fumble, turnover, or confusion. The passer (a handoff is a pass) has the lead hand on top of the ball with the lead elbow up and the back hand under the ball. That technique discourages the defender from trying to fight over the top and blow up the handoff. The receiver takes the handoff with both hands on the sides of the ball. We introduced this fundamental in our basic passing drill on pages 20 and 21.

Whether on the ball or off, the art of the screen and roll is reminiscent of two elite dancers in excellent rhythm. They seem to know what the other is thinking; they read the defense as one unit. One example of that togetherness in the execution of this basketball basic is the following: The screener is usually blind to what the defense is doing from behind because vision is set on setting a good screen on one defensive player. The offensive player to be screened can see what is behind the screener. The verbal, "Bump," from the player to be screened is a possible command for the screener to slip instead of setting the ball screen. That example is just one of many possibilities, so once again, taking what the defense gives is essential.

Finally, beating a defender off any type of screen, on or off the ball, requires both hip and shoulder brushing low around the screen. If the screen and roll and its many types are to be executed correctly, lots of 1-on-1 and 3-on-3 are prime tools for training, reading defenses, verbal and visual communication, and good teamwork.

5. The Five Principles of Balance

These principles are a must for teaching players at summer camps, no matter the age, then reinforcing early in the regular season.

- Head splits distance between legs.

- Legs are wider than shoulders.

- Weight is on the inside of the balls of the feet.

- Players' legs are in mid-stance: not too high and not too low. Quite similar to Goldilocks's porridge-not too hot nor too cold-just right! This stance is an unnatural position and players have to become used to it.

- Chin is parallel to the floor.

6. Stopping, Starting, and Pivoting

In basketball, a high percentage of all turnovers are the result of errors in footwork. Players must be educated and drilled for mastery in these areas. The game is not played at a continuous speed. It is a series of quick stops, starts, and pivots. Whether in summer camp or at a December practice, some degree of attention must be made to continuous improvement in player footwork. In any offense, footwork is fundamental to success. Players must be educated and drilled in this area.

STOPPING

Instruct and drill both the 1-2 stop and the two-foot jump stop. Emphasize heel-to-toe on all stops for better balance.

STARTING

Instruct and drill both the long jab step and the short jab (six-inch quick jab at front foot of defender). Add the dribble from both the onside start and crossover.

PIVOTING

Keep a mid-stance. Instruct both an inside and an outside pivot. Keep the ball at the chin unless faking high or low. Be ready to shoot or at least be an offensive threat.

Getting open to receive a pass requires a knowledge of how you are being guarded and by whom. Whether it's a tight man, a packed in zone, a box and one, or any other defensive coverage, the offensive player always has one huge advantage. The offense knows when the race starts. The closer the offensive player is to the defender decreases the amount of reaction time the defender has to respond to a quick change of speed or direction. This applies to almost all moves to get open: coming off a screen, using a simple V or L cut on the wing, receiving a handoff, back cutting an overplaying defender, or flair cutting on a defender who goes under a screen, etc. Many times, an offense's best scorers must put several combinations of these moves together to find the opening. Another great way to get open is to set a screen to force the defender to help or even screen a screener. This motion causes communication challenges for the defense.

As a general rule, most cuts are preceded by a counter or misdirection step to either make defenders lose sight of their assignment or lose the position to react. If a defender loses sight of the ball in the effort to guard a player, eye, head, and hand fakes are also useful. Correct starting, stopping, and pivoting each plays a role in both getting open and receiving a pass basketball-ready.

7. Role Definition

Players need to understand their strengths and limitations; in effect, learn their mental, physical, and emotional discomfort levels. By accepting their individual responsibilities on a team, they can learn to be "stars" in their own roles. They also need to know ways that their strengths contribute to a team's success and affect a game's outcome. Bi-weekly individual meetings with players are essential to help define their roles on the team and for welfare checks about their attitude and grades. Defining a player's role does not limit a player's contributions; the roles simplify the game for the player and help build confidence. Roles also build better communication with the coach. Many players (and their parents) focus primarily about playing time. If players fulfill their roles, playing time can be a non-issue. The better the player fulfills a role, the more progress that player has the chance to make. Trust=playing time; smart coaches play players they trust. One day, players will belong to organizations for employment. They will have roles to play. Furthermore, roles help players understand that a team is not a democracy. Inequality exists. Not everyone is the star, nor is everyone a best player, nor are certain players the starters. Players learn that they have a role to play for a team's success. What relevant connections to life. In short, be invaluable without necessarily being most valuable!

 REFLECTION

TOM McCORMACK

After a nice high school career and a terrific senior season as our point guard and leader, my son Pat was attending a D-3 college and playing the backup point guard spot to a very skilled, athletic teammate. As the season progressed and although he initially didn't start, Pat played most of the last five or more minutes of close games. Ever notice how a team's sixth man can wind up finishing the majority of close games on the court? Coach Red Auerbach was one of the first coaches to recognize the importance of this role. Trust has everything to do with who the finishers are.

8. Guarding the Ball

THE toughest part of becoming a good defender. Can players contain the basketball off the dribble and contest the shot? Can they keep themselves in front of the ball? Can they "guard a yard"? Can they deflect passes or strip the ball? These precious defensive skills are all done on the ground. Teaching players the correct movement with their feet (outside foot lifts in direction of the first dribble) is essential. Determination and toughness are more essential. There is much more about defense in the Guts chapter.

9. Talking at Both Ends

Why do we include the voice? Very few players use their vocal cords at both ends of the court. Talking is an essential asset for any good team. The teams that talk, care. Coaches should teach a one-syllable vocabulary for necessary vocal communication. Some examples are "GO" for a defensive rebounding to start the break, "GAP" for proper position off the ball on defense, "LOOSE" for loose balls, "SHOT" for the opponent's attempt, "HERE" for post player to call for the ball, etc. "Early, loud," and "often" are the three keys for any team that communicates well.

 REFLECTION

TOM ANSTETT

Living in Green Bay, Wisconsin, I have watched the St. Norbert College men's basketball team. Head coach Gary Grzesk and his staff are experts at teaching and demanding his players to excel at the defensive end of the court. Coach Grzesk was a tenacious defender during his college days at U-W-Green Bay, and as (the late) Marquette University coach Al McGuire once said, "Coaches coach as they played." I marvel at the St. Norbert College players' consistent talking on defense on most every possession. I have watched occasional practices too, and they practice what they preach. Correct it or accept it.

10. Attitude

There is a reason for "Attitude" being #10. It is the foundation for the afore-mentioned nine skills. Without good attitude, what can really be accomplished, whether in basketball or in life? Bill Russell of the Boston Celtics states in his book, Russell Rules, "Create unselfishness as the most important team attribute." Ever watch Division-III basketball? Those players, like many high school hoopsters, play for the love of the game. There are no scholarships, very little television time, and few after-the-game hordes of reporters jamming microphones into coaches' and players' faces. Just the love of the game. This love stems from unselfishness, arguably the most valuable trait of winning programs and their players. One might witness unselfishness at the defensive end of the court when players take charges, dive for loose balls, talk on defense every possession, make the sprint back on defense when all seems lost, check on teammates who miss practice or are ill, or run to a fallen teammate to help him or her up after a collision. On offense, don't we admire the extra pass or the player who willingly gives up his/her body to set as many screens as possible? Moreover, when a player scored, we only allowed that scorer to point a finger at the teammate who passed the ball. No showboating or gesticulating to the crowd. Just get back on defense, ready to go. Unselfishness has to be discussed and valued within a program. When it happens on game film or in practice, recognition or praise is a good follow-up. Is it just us or is this trait witnessed more often on the freshman level, disappearing from view more readily as players age? How is unselfishness valued in your program?

 REFLECTION

TOM ANSTETT

Progress? You want to know progress? In my sophomore year, my first one playing basketball, I was 6'3" and had as much muscle as the 96-pound weakling on a beach. The basketball was a foreign object. Progress that season was my understanding which basket I could shoot at. When tired, I needed directions. No joke. I did score for the opponent once in a November scrimmage. My ability to maintain a level of play against good teams was my measurement for progress the next season. Because I had locked myself in a gym for three hours every night that summer after working during the day for my dad, I averaged 27 points per game the following winter. Senior year my goal was to dominate opponents. In one game I had 27 rebounds. In another I scored 51 points. I was All-State in Illinois. Between and among all those numbers and accomplishments were lots of blood, sweat, and tears with a heavy dose of relentlessness from my high school coach, Bill Schaefer. During all that preparation, I never quite understood what was happening to me. Call it naivete or a lack of appreciation from a typical teenager. As time progressed, however, the clarity for the importance of preparation crystalized. Thereafter, I applied it to many aspects of my life, including classroom teaching and parenting.

SOME "A-B-Cs..." FOR PREPARATION

A. Always Challenge the Best Players

Entitlement for these players is a recipe for disaster as the season progresses. If entitlement starts to creep into a team, dissention is not far away. It's okay for players to verbally "critique" other players, but never for something they don't do themselves. Former NBA coach and current analyst Jeff van Gundy said, "If your best player is also your hardest worker, you've really got something." Competing in everything, every day, especially at practice is the key. How often is your most talented player the first to the floor for a loose ball, a leader in conditioning, or the first to pick up a cup or towel off the floor? As the head coach we always made it a point to sweep the floor before practice, so the players saw a model of non-entitlement behavior. We made a game of it. During pre-practice, if they ever ran into us with the mop or their errant shot ever hit us in the head, they had to finish sweeping.

The better players are often the seniors. They have the most experience and should have the most skill and acumen for the game. Challenging the best players with corrective detail in drills and with toughness is paramount to a team's progress. The best players do what is required in the moment, not what they feel like doing. The best players are sound defensive players. They know what the coach wants. Furthermore, if the best players are consistently challenged at practice, that example to the younger players is invaluable. We wanted the younger players to be able to watch the seniors and/or the better players for models on hard work and effort. We wanted the younger players to say to themselves, "That is what I want to be."

At the beginning, middle, and end of a season. the players took an anonymous paper vote in three categories: Best Player, Hardest Worker, and Best Teammate. We posted the results for the players in our meeting room. It was pretty accurate that when our best players scored high in all three categories, we had some enjoyable seasons. These votes often recognized a few of the players who received little playing time by being ranked high in the "hardest worker" or "best teammate" categories. Conversely, the rankings opened the eyes of any prima donna who was one of the better players, but not seen in the eyes of teammates as a particularly hard worker or good teammate.

The best way to keep entitlement from a team lies in the culture of the program. Two important points here are off-season work and the practice culture. The better players need to be constantly challenged in competitive drills that declare a winner. Putting the better players at a competitive disadvantage or distorting the drill or scrimmage are two examples. Distorting might encompass giving the second team three points instead of two for a two-point basket and four points instead of three for a 3-pointer. Perhaps the only way the first group can win is the number of defensive stops. There are all kinds of ways to alter the game so that the first group has to work harder in order to improve, and the best players have to play and lead better.

B. Bring those Notebooks

As head coaches, we insisted on players keeping individual notebooks. These records helped player-coach communication, self-evaluation, scouting, and offensive movements. Notebooks are signs of caring and dedication. Coaches can devise or organize notebooks in various ways. The point is for players to document the team's and their own progress. The pro golfer Curtis Strange remarked, "If I do not evaluate myself, I don't really care."

 REFLECTION

TOM ANSTETT

I had my players write weekly evaluations of practices, including their own progress on offense and defense. I taught them how to set specific goals; from that instruction, they wrote a daily goal for offense, defense, and attitude. They wrote a short evaluation for each goal. They could keep the same three goals for the entire week, if preferred. I also had them use a part of the notebook for scouting reports. These notebooks recorded their summer work also. I considered the notebooks part of the equipment for practice. If a player forgot it, there was a penalty. One summer at camp, I had a player run back to his house to retrieve his notebook before he practiced. Players and I used them for individual conferences, conducted at least bi-weekly. I discovered a great deal through these conferences about a player's background, attitude, his play, or his emotional status, reasons he was practicing well or not, etc. They also helped me evaluate the team's progress through the players' perspectives. Writing is thinking.

REFLECTION

TOM McCORMACK

After our third day of tryouts, we gave each player on the team a two-pocket folder with a spiral notebook and a monthly calendar listing the game and practice schedule. At every team meeting or film and scouting report session, each player was responsible to bring his folder. Any information discussed was written in the notebook, similar to notetaking in an academic class. It was also a place to file printed information like scouting reports or diagrams we distributed. Periodically, we had the players write their own reflections on a certain topic in the notebook, usually, but not always, basketball related. We made it clear that the folder was as important as the same types of instruments they applied to their academic classes. Lou Carnesecca, the former coach at St. John's University, called the area where they held their team meetings the "classroom" and the practice court the "laboratory."

C. Cultivate the Coaching Staff

Putting together a coaching staff and maximizing its talents are both primary duties and talents. Many factors go into choosing a staff, but loyalty is the first and foremost. A head coach should give some consideration to hiring responsible former players as assistants. Those people know the coach and the system and bring a unique perspective to the program. Often, the current players in the program admired those alumni as players. Of course, a head coach wants assistants who think similarly but also are willing to play the devil's advocate. There can be disagreement without being disagreeable. However, once a decision is made by the head coach, everyone must be on board.

Disagree without being disagreeable

Placement of coaches at the various levels is crucial. Head coaches should always take into consideration the assistants' preferences. "I would really like to be…, but I'll do whatever the program needs," is a desirable answer to receive when the head coach discusses placement with assistants. The head freshman coach needs to understand the fundamentals with an ability to teach those skills and possess an enthusiastic personality to hook players into wanting to give four years into a program, provided that the player has the skills to do so and is willing to supply the dedication. The assistant freshman position, the "B" coach, is a good spot for an inexperienced coach. "B" games have less pressure, so the novice coach can grow without being under a huge microscope. The sophomore coach, or JV if there is no sophomore level, needs to operate very similarly to the varsity in practice and game situations. Sophomore year is a key decision year for players concerning their commitment to the program. The sophomore coach should guide and push players toward that decision. The assistant varsity coach needs to complement the head coach's strengths and personality. On the other hand, this coach has a responsibility to offer disagreement and/or an opposite viewpoint, so that the head coach receives a complete picture for practices, for a game plan, and for other factors. A second varsity assistant spot is a good place for a new coach with aspirations to advance and a willingness to learn. Moreover, any good assistant rarely hands problems over to the head coach. A valuable assistant tries to extinguish fires before the head coach has to deal with a distraction that takes away from the head coach's coaching, teaching, and planning time. It's even better if the assistant can stop issues before they happen or become bigger problems than they should be. This personal skill takes someone who has in mind the big picture of what is best for the program, not just for one team in the program.

Three qualities are ideal for an assistant. First is a love for the game. Second is a willingness to keep learning. This willingness can transpire into the desire to one day becoming a head coach. These coaches are usually highly motivated teachers and learners and seek quality and precision. Third is the ability to show the necessary reliance and toughness during rough or unpleasant times. Playing and previous coaching experience can be assets but are far from being pre-requisites. Some outstanding coaches have had little to no playing experience. A possible drawback to having a great basketball playing career for coaches is to have the irrational push for players to be as good as they were. That mentality distorts a coach's vision for players and can alter the approach to players' mistakes and the ability to communicate with the team.

Assistant positions can be filled with volunteers, too, especially for candidates with a teaching position that the administration desires. If you are unsure of a prospective hire as an assistant coach, consider asking that individual to volunteer without pay for a season. Eventually, that person will reveal his/her motivation and priorities.

All coaches need to know and share the philosophy of both the program and their specific level assignment. Assistants who work for the head coach are important, but assistants who work with the head coach produce rewards and fun. People who work for someone often have limits and self-promoting motives. People who work with someone have the pride of ownership and will go the extra mile for the team. Freshman and sophomore levels are primarily responsible for player development, not winning. Competing to win is part of life and sports. However, everyone's main responsibility is to do what is necessary at their particular level to develop players for the varsity and develop in players the needed people skills for their life's work, whatever that work might be. Teaching ability, communication skills, problem solving, and enthusiasm go a long way for any coach. Each talent is a strong model for players and a worthy goal for becoming a good coach. Visibility of those models creates credibility.

Head Coaches' Responsibilities to their Assistants

Head coaches must conduct a two-way street for communication and loyalty and make clear the expectations and responsibilities. Everyone makes mistakes and a good coach admits them, finds a way to fix them, and then follows through by fixing the mistakes, or at the very least, learns from those errors. Assistant coaches and players will see right through a head coach who blames others too readily for personal weaknesses or poor decisions. When accepting credit, the head coach should use "we" and "us" after a victory and use singular pronouns like "myself" and "I" after a loss. This specific vocabulary also applies to accepting praise ("we" and "us") or criticism ("myself" and "I").

The following list supplies ideas for the head coach to consider as his/her responsibilities to assistants:

- Make very clear their duties in and out of season and hold assistants accountable.

- Explain and teach to assistants the fundamental skills with the specific techniques for instruction to players, drill work, Xs & Os, game strategies etc., and provide the required training for any levels, especially anything new. There could be a big range in assistants' levels of competence, experience, and motivation. These explanations provide great fodder for pre-season meetings that promote preparation.

- Encourage professional development through access to coaching clinics, skill and training videos, college practice and games, etc.

- Make it clear that some of the best training they can acquire is to attend varsity practice whenever possible. Next is attendance at varsity games if this is not already an assigned duty.

- Hold regular (weekly, if possible) coaches' meetings for all levels.

- Be sensitive to assistants' responsibilities: family, teaching load, etc. These should be reviewed and agreed to before offering and/ or accepting a coaching position. The unexpected can always occur, but distractions of any sort by coaches or players are detrimental to a team.

- For assistants who aspire to be head coaches, guide and recommend those coaches toward achieving that goal, if those candidates earn that recommendation.

- Instruct assistants ways to deal with the press after a game. Focus the positives on the players and also mention an assistant who might have prepared the scouting report or assisted with the game plan. Anything negative that must be addressed should be done with only team members present and kept within that confine.

- Let your assistants and administration know what is acceptable and what is not to discuss with parents. Playing time, game strategy, and discussing other players were off limits. Academics, behavior, improvement suggestions, off-season trainers and teams, playing after high school etc., are all appropriate topics to discuss, but be aware parents will often use these, especially the first three, as a back door to try to discuss playing time or game strategy.

- Model behavior and work ethic. A little humility goes a long way with players and other coaches. One example: As head coaches we had a routine of sweeping the gym floor before practices in full view of the assistants, managers, and players. Translation: no task is too small to take pride in doing well. From time to time but not often, let assistant coaches and players see the side of you come out when duties and responsibilities are not met. At some point, human nature will take advantage of the nice guy. You don't want to cross the motivational line from respect to fear. Direct honesty is the best form of fairness. Let each party know where it stands.

- Provide direction as to what is proper and what is not with assistants' relationships with players. Head coaches come with all types of personalities, but there needs to be a line. If a correction is necessary, one on one is usually the best way. If the situation is sensitive for both the assistant coach or player, both another assistant and the head coach should be present to avoid exaggeration in the future.

- Try to hire the most talented assistants possible. Many high school coaching and assistant coaching positions are attached with academic responsibilities. Head coaches are not always able to hire the strongest coaching candidate because a teaching position and coaching position have to fit together.

- Help assistants realize that while coaching expertise, drill work, and game coaching are important, these pieces are only a portion of their duties and responsibilities. Just like the players, the most talented assistants need to be team players.

- Face-to-face communication is more desirable than text messages or emails.

- Help assistants and players understand that popularity is nice, but respect is the key to staying power and long-term success. The peace of mind that comes with doing the job right comes with the willingness to lose the job based on principles. Selling out on the non-negotiables is a non-negotiable. That foible marks the beginning of the end and supplies plenty of self-doubt, a hard adversary. Avoid too many rules that can't be applied equally, or an administration will be reluctant to support the program. Win or lose, sleep becomes a problem when compromise overwhelms self-discipline and vision. As Benjamin Franklin once noted, "There's no pillow as soft as a clear conscience."

Assistant Coaches' Responsibilities

Assistants need to understand that whether on the court or in the classroom, they are teachers first. That being said, coaches have a motivational advantage over the classroom teacher. The vast majority of players choose to be there; this choice is not always the case in the classroom. As stated earlier, coaching, teaching, and planning time are crucial at all levels. Head coaches need to delegate to assistants the tasks that interfere with these primary tasks. Some assignments will be challenging and exciting; some will be tedious and boring. It is often the quality, thoroughness, and punctuality of these types of tasks that reveal the true worth of a good assistant. One principle job of an assistant is to keep the head coach sane. No matter how good assistants are, they will never feel the pressure the head coach feels. However, they can dissipate some of that pressure.

Here is a list of possible tasks for assistants:

- Organize, compile, and print the season's practice and game schedules for all levels.

- Direct or assist fundraising events.

- Because assistant coaches can afford to get closer to players than the head coach, they should offer information that the head coach might not know.

- Supervise open gyms.

- Run pre-season conditioning sessions.

- Assist in budget planning.

- Assistants need to understand that whether on the court or in the classroom, they are teachers first.

- Be responsible for managing video equipment and personnel.

- Direct or assist and teach/coach summer camps and youth clinics.

- Direct or present topics at coaches' clinics for area youth coaches.

- Organize and attend summer leagues and tournaments.

- Organize the in-season scouting schedule. Perhaps obtain film and tech information on opponents. Every coach in the program can be assigned to scout one conference and at least one non-conference team on the schedule. That coach then attends the meeting to prepare for that opponent and presents the scouting report and ideas for a game plan. This task gives them a feeling of importance and makes doing the other less glamorous tasks easier.

- Check in with players on their off-season workouts. Make suggestions and encourage.

- Set up pre-season player and parent meetings and overview the expectations.

- Communicate to set up a positive relationship with the training staff.

- Keep track of players' academic progress and behavior. Stay in touch with teachers and administrators. Try to head off problems.

- Help the head coach take care of tasks like rules meetings, officials' ratings, eligibility lists, state association requirements, etc.

- Compile statistical info.

- Recruit, train, and encourage potential managers. Make them a part of the team and invaluable to a program.

- Keep an eye in the hallways. Spot a tall kid or a great athlete in gym class that just needs a little encouragement. Some don't pan out, but every once in a while, there is a diamond in the rough. What's the shoe size?

- Be humble enough to accept direction from the head coach regarding player development. For example, a freshman "A" coach might have a big player who is slow or a bit unskilled, so the freshman coach does not use that player much. The big player has good potential, however. Height cannot be taught. If the head coach wants that player to get more minutes, swallow the pride and play that athlete more. Development at that age and level outweighs winning. Coaching lives is as essential as coaching players.

- Keep inventory and be responsible for equipment.

- After tryouts, conduct individual meetings with all players both kept and cut. This is not fun, but a must. The players who made the team need to understand this is not the "everybody gets a trophy" world anymore. Informing players who do not make the team must be done with some compassion and some realistic encouragement. It is best to have more than one coach present for these meetings.

 REFLECTION

TOM McCORMACK

At a clinic I attended as a young assistant, an assistant coach gave some advice to the assistant coaches present, specifically to varsity assistants. He said, "Never let the second team you're coaching beat the first team in a scrimmage. It just pisses off the head coach, and you'll never get out of there." (Coaches Abe Lemons and Bill White, University of Texas). When I was an assistant, the head coach and I often played H-O-R-S-E or 1-on-1 after practice or in the afternoon before a game. I let him win once in a while for the same reason.

"The 18-inch move on the bench from assistant to head coach makes all the difference in the world." That statement by former DePaul head coach Joey Meyer was a response to a question about the difference between being a head coach and an assistant. Joey was his dad's (Ray Meyer) assistant for 11 years before his 18-inch move.

D. Develop the Lower Levels

Organize a "Big-Brother" program. Pair up varsity players with two or three players from the lower levels. If the facilities allow, practice together as a program once a week for an hour. Stations are a good structure. The head coach or assistant might give a short talk about a pertinent topic. Maybe the entire program can watch some game film together. On occasion, have those groups talk together for a short time about practice progress, ways to play harder, questions, etc.

We wanted our freshmen and sophomore/J-V at all home games sitting as a group behind the varsity bench. Road games were harder to do that. Another concept we employed was a buddy system where the players are not only responsible for themselves, but also for another player on the team. For example, teaming a more responsible player with a less responsible one is a dynamic worth considering.

E. Excel with Scouting

Scouting is a coach's decision in terms of its form and its value. Bob Knight repeatedly said he did not scout much because he focused solely on his players' ability to play a "perfect game." He felt if his players competed to their best against the game itself, the outcome took care of itself. For the majority of coaches, however, scouting is a necessity and a time-consuming task. Coaches must also encourage players to understand its importance. Scouting is never busywork.

A prime responsibility for assistant coaches at practice, other than organizing and conducting drill and conditioning segments, is preparing the scout team and providing the first unit the best look possible on the offenses, defenses, and special situations of the upcoming opponent. Those players have to be immersed in this vital importance. These players understand that they might not play a second in the game, yet their contributions at practice and on the bench during the actual game are critical to each outcome.

At practice an assistant coach took the scout team to assign roles and work on the game plan for the upcoming opponent. Imitating the other team's best player is a role that can develop an inexperienced player on the scout team. Sometimes there are non-playing seniors or a player who is one of those special kids always giving maximum effort and positive attitude. Consider making one of those players the captain of the scout unit and the assistant coach's right hand. Having an invested scout team makes practices more challenging and competitive. Preparing for an opponent by keeping the intensity level high at practice and maintaining alertness and enthusiasm on the bench are a successful program's staples and contribute to the growth of the program. Job security for the first team players should not change much, especially on a cohesive team, but it should be constantly challenged and evaluated each week.

We often mentioned the contributions of the scout team to the press after a victory. On occasion, players will perform so well on the scout team that they have an opportunity to move into the playing rotation. Furthermore, we had many players come from the scout team as juniors to vital roles in the playing rotation as seniors.

In-Person Scouting

Scouting a team in person and taking notes requires a high level of concentration because there is no replay. It is possible, however, to pick up some details a camera might miss. Sometimes a coach/scout might want to just watch the game and get the overall big picture without note taking. If you are taking notes, we suggest a pre-printed form that makes it more efficient to write, then get your attention back to the action.

Scouting From Video or Film

Because of its ability to replay, freeze frame, and edit, video scouting has become a tremendous tool. Coaches can pinpoint the exactness of the execution and personnel but can lose perspective on things like the actual size, attentiveness, and frustration levels of the opponent's players. Some scouts today will watch a game with a camera recording and try to accomplish both types at once.

Once the scout is completed, coaches evaluate the amount and the type of information required. We suggest a separate and compartmentalized form from the one used to live scout or break down the video. This detail is presented to the coaches and players. This form can be done via hard copy or on a device such as an iPad.

The coaches' meeting is the time to put the information together and decide the manner it will be given to the team. Sometimes there is enough time to both review a scouting report and practices. For other games a chalk talk is all that is possible.

The players' meeting to study the scouting report needs astute organization. It's a good idea for coaches to ask questions during the meeting to maintain alertness since the maturity level and attention span of players are erratic and unpredictable. If the scout is a video, specific editing saves time and helps absorption of the key points. If playing an opponent for a second or a third time, the best scout video is probably of the previous game with that opponent. Some new wrinkles are in order though, especially if the first game was a win.

Consider the storage of the scouting instruments. One suggestion is a folder and notebook for players to store hard copies or notes taken from a chalk/white board. Establish a folder section for tech storage on computers and iPad. Put the player's names and numbers on all folders, notebooks, and distributed materials. All team members must realize that this information can never be lost, misplaced, or given out in any way. Once in a while, coaches might be fortunate enough to find a scouting report on their own team. It is interesting to see the reactions of the players when they read how other coaches have described them as individual players and the descriptions of the team. Putting the players' names and numbers on these materials serves to hold everyone accountable. Players are responsible to have their folders, notebooks, or iPad at team meetings.

In the end, the result of any scouting is decision making. Coaches evaluate what they observe and make decisions for game preparation and desired execution. Scouting decisions are a team effort by the coaching staff. Opposing teams can exchange video, so each coach gets more than one look. Seeing an upcoming opponent at least twice is beneficial. Watching one game in their home gym and the same team on the road provides a more complete picture of team and individual tendencies.

More ideas for consideration:

- Scouting can be a responsibility for an assistant coach. That coach can review a scout before a game. Whoever has the role, a scouting schedule is advisable.

- As technology increases its capability, coaches should evaluate any new uses within scouting. The use of Hudl or other comparable technology is one example.

- Head coach may want to attend games with their new coaches, so they can teach their staff exactly what they are looking for and how to scout.

- Players learn by means of visual, auditory, or kinetic forms. Thus, film work, walk-throughs, and talk-throughs cover all three.

- A useful form of scouting is to acquire a scouting report done on your own team by a capable observer in practices or games. Three times throughout one season are desirable (early, mid, and late season).

- Coaches have to consider the amount of practice time devoted to implementation of a scouting report.

- When does a coach give a copy of a scouting report to the players? early in the week? the day before? in pre-game so players can review before the warm-up? as take-home material?

- A one-page scouting report template must be prepared with the key points for decision-making. Players can only synthesize so much material. It is more essential that they get themselves ready to play.

- Bus rides to and from games are important team time. If the ride is long, some relaxation is in order. If the trip is short, that time offers discussion of various aspects of the game plan. In either case, we discouraged use of headphones or earbuds. We wanted the players talking basketball with each other. Also, in terms of traveling on overnight trips, coaches have to be very aware of schedules outside of game time. Curfews and assigning of assistants to monitor players are essential pieces to planning those trips. One way to look at it: if players bug the head coach about going on overnight trips, one response might be, "Get us downstate. Then we will stay overnight."

See the following samples for an actual report and essential questions.

Sample: Essential Scouting Questions

Here are six sets of questions to observe when scouting an opponent, then discussing to determine preparation:

1. In our M2M defense, who guards whom? Which player(s) can we shade and not guard closely?

   In our zone defense, who are the two best outside shooters to shade?

2. How does the opponent respond to pressure? What type?

   What press(es) do(es) the opponent use? How do we attack that pressure?

3. How good is their point guard? What can we do to contain him/her or take him/her out of their offense?

4. What are their special plays or last-second sets? Who are their key players in these sets?

   What are the baseline out of bounds plays? How effective are they?

5. What are our keys to victory?

   What things do we need to cover in practice before we play them?

6. How precise is your report on individuals? Perimeter players: favor which hand? favorite move? favorite spots for a shot? Post players: What moves do they use? Which shoulder should we take away? Should we guard one-on-one or swarm?

Sample: Completed Scouting Report

Courtesy of coach Rich Kolimas at Lincoln-Way East High School in Frankfort, IL

SCOUTING REPORT

STARTERS

#10   Andrew Flanagan   6'0" Sr
~Role player—3 pt. shooter

#20   Jacob Karli   5'11" So
~Very good outside shooter—must closeout and contest;
seems to like the right wing
~Many inbounds plays are for him—left corner

#1   Matt Smietanski   6'0" Sr
~Very good post feeder
~Drives well vs. man or zone from the wing
~Finishes well inside
~Capable from 3 and good pull-up jumper
~Very good FT shooter—keep off the line

#3   Christian Schultz   6'6" Sr—LEFTY!
~Long, lanky
~Good rebounder
~Becoming more a threat offensively

#42   John Meyer   6'6" Jr
~Big body, wide—have to box out
~Primary post option—finishes strong inside
~No left hand
~Posts hard and seals well—very active
~Sets good screens—yell Red on ball screen

BENCH

#4   Patrick Cooper   6'0" Sr
~Athletic/slasher
~Capable from 3—especially top of key
~Understands his role, mainly a facilitator

#24   Chase Travis   6'3" Sr
~Long, athletic—good leaper
~Good finisher around rim—finishes strong
~Good rebounder—must keep a body on him
~Looks to post up—pick n roll with #1 too

#12   Matt Medina   6'5" Sr—LEFTY
~Strong build
~Posts strong on the block
~Tendency to play out of control at times
~Will make poor decisions if pressured
~Lowers his shoulder—draw an offensive foul

OFFENSE
  Secondary
      lob for #3 or #24 or America's Play from left side vs. M2M
      "Eagle"—flex into America play
      "Corner"—#1 on clear out right side
      "1" high ball screen for #1
      "Double Fist"
      dribble hand offs
      shallow downscreens for 3-point shooters top of key

  vs. Zone
      "Thumbs Down"—Bengal with rotation high post
      "Triangle" = 3 out on top, 2 post on baseline—watch for a
        baseline cross-screen

  Under OBs (no calls)
      Our 24 look initially, ends in a baseline double-screen for #1
      Screen-the-screener action w/ #42 ending up on the weak-side
      block

  Secondary
      Backscreen lob to weakside—Strongside post up

DEFENSE
     Matchup 2-3 zone (will extend)
         2-3 zone under OB
     "22" = 2-2-1 — ¾ court
     "5" = M2M (switch at times)

KEYS TO VICTORY
     Take away their inside game
     Help on drives, esp. #1
     Move the ball on offense—hit the open man
     Find a way

F. FINE-TUNE PRACTICE

When considering practice, coaches need to ask and answer: What is the culture we desire, with culture defined as the way we do things? Practice organization and correct habits are the heart of the matter. We provide examples of practice organization, a flow chart for the progress of the players, checklists for preparation, and an example of a season breakdown. In reality, the more and the better the players can coach each other, the more progress a program makes.

 REFLECTION

TOM McCORMACK

A typical in-season practice routine was pre-practice direction, warm-up, individual or group defense, individual or group offense, team defense, team offense, scrimmage, and post-practice reflection. The time of season determined the type and duration of conditioning during practices. We tried to do most of our in-season conditioning in competitive drill work for a goal and reward or penalty. Off-season work included all the same but emphasized individual improvement work. In any practice make sure your system of offense matches your system of defense.

 REFLECTION

TOM ANSTETT

Frankly, I enjoyed practices as much as games. I relished seeing players improve by applying what they learned and drilled in practices and transferring those improvements to games. Practice planning was dependent on the time of season. Practice plans were posted for players before they came onto the court. This plan included a quote for practice which they were required to memorize and an emphasis for that practice. All practices included five pieces other than warm-up: necessary fundamentals (always with shooting), team defense, team offense, transition work, last-second prep. The team offense and defense meant game planning from Tuesday to Thursday with Friday games.

One key question for all coaches: Are you married to the plan? In other words, once the time for a certain drill is up, do you move ahead, no matter how poorly the team might be doing that drill or do you stay with that drill until you're happy? There are advantages to both. My suggestion is to make a short competition for the team at the end of a drill, especially if it is being poorly executed. Of course, you might have planned a competitive ending anyway.

Practice always began with a brief team meeting at center court with conversation about the plan for the day, the quote, and a short motivation. Warm-up was led by captains with ten stretches and/or pre-practice. Warm-up included jump rope for five minutes. Ball handling was done before any shooting. Practice organization included offensive work with position breakdowns (perimeter and post at least twice a week) and team prep for upcoming opponent from Tuesday through Thursday. Mondays were a "repair the weekend" day, unless we had a Tuesday game.

Prime Practice Points

- Coaches should make practices harder than games.

- Whether or not the shot clock is in effect, there are some basic physical and cerebral skills high school players must execute, with shot selection becoming a vital element.

- The Three Amigos: Make no excuses. Expect nothing. Do something.

- This bears repeating: Is the system fitting the players or do players have to fit the system?

- Players practice shooting without a ball, so correct technique is the main focus. The ball is a distraction when practicing shooting form; players are too concerned with the ball going in, instead of the process by which it will go in. This type of drill is best practiced in the early season and in the off-season but can be a brief part of every warm-up for practice.

- How well is the second team motivated to practice hard and to improve? This consideration becomes more important as the season progresses.

- Coaches, does every drill contain skills used in games? If not, this is akin to a classroom teacher assigning students to read a certain text without supplying a specific focus for reading. Players need to see why they are doing what you instruct. People don't buy what you do; they buy why you do it. This explanation helps coaches' credibility and their own knowledge of the game.

- After the team is decided, coaches must plan a portion of every practice for last-second situations. Players enjoy this part of practice due to the competition of the game itself. There is a ton to teach. Coaches will detect certain players who might fulfill a key role; for example, the team is losing, and one particular player has the guts and ability to deny a man the ball and force turnovers. Which player wants the ball in crunch time?

- Proposal: If the freshman level has two teams, have the freshmen coaches switch teams periodically. This change promotes interchangeable players with a feeling of equity that there is one freshmen team. One coach does not monopolize the best players on an "A" team; thus, players are evaluated by more than one coach. Healthy for everyone.

- Although the practice routine is divided into specific segments and progressions of defensive and offensive work, much of the drill work in all the segments should include elements of both. This combination enhances more efficient use of time, player involvement and activity, and competitiveness. There are times when specific things need to be addressed and drilled solely by an individual. An example is a particular shot mechanic or pivoting action. However, most drill work, even though it may emphasize a certain defensive or offensive technique or fundamental, is most efficiently accomplished with elements of both.

- A tempting point can come at the end of practice. We all try to have practice end on a high note, but sometimes things are just not going well. The players might lack execution or intensity level. If the gym is still available at the scheduled end time of practice, do you stay there till you get it right or end practice? No matter how practice has progressed, we found that trying to squeeze in a couple more reps at the end of practice often led to fatigue or frustration injuries. We suggest ending practice at the scheduled time, conduct a brief meeting to identify any issues, and return to it tomorrow.

PRE-Practice, Anyone?

IDEA #1:

Prepare and organize a "pre-practice" as part of warm-up. This type of practice routine emphasizes those three essentials Carril mentions. Run an eight-station series consisting of physical development (jump ropes), defensive slides, chair drill (working on post triple threat with ball in chair), free throws, 3-point shooting, passing, dribbling, and post work.

IDEA #2:

Vary this routine with eight-station shooting and dribbling sets. The stations might be 3-point shooting, free throw shooting, mid-range shooting off pass, mid-range off the dribble, form shooting, pull-back crossover dribble, change of pace dribble, and one dribble move into a layup. Each layup should be shot differently: reverse, off two feet, etc.

IDEA #3:

Are you pinpointing the fundamentals within the team drills you conduct during every practice? For example, when a turnover is committed, are you teaching why the turnover was committed with a fundamental concept? In that way, players see reasons and connection to drills in practice that isolate the fundamentals. They will work harder. They understand the why. If they do not yet understand it, explain it again.

Checklist for Defense Preparation

- Half-court defense
- Out of bounds baseline defense
- Out of bounds sideline defense
- Press defense
- Trap defense

- Fouling to stop the clock situations and technique

- End clock and game situations

- Transition defense responsibilities

Defensive Free Throw Situations & Huddle

- 1 shot, 1+ 1 bonus, 2 shots, 3 shots: The defensive players alternate sides from the top two spots after each attempt. Walk slowly; distract the shooter; throw off the rhythm.

Jump Ball Situations (Defense and Offense)

OFFENSE

PHILOSOPHY: (Light?) years ago when authors Tom and Tom played, we had two guards, two forwards, and one center. We now have player numbers and position-less players. Without endorsing any specific offensive pattern or system, the two basic choices are continuity (patterns and set plays) or motion (playing by principles of reading the defense and reacting). Some offensive systems combine concepts from both. The advantage of continuity lies in the specifics of execution. Continuity appeals to a team's specific strengths but not necessarily to one individual or to the best players. There will be options getting from point A to point B that are easy to grasp for most of the team. Typically, the options require different sets for different defenses, so players have to learn several. It is not difficult to scout. When a good executing continuity team goes up against a solid and prepared defensive team, the game becomes a battle of wills.

Motion systems, on the other hand, rely on player reaction to what the defense presents. There are more options to read, and roles within the offense are more defined. Motion coaches have said, "The great thing about motion is that it is so unpredictable, and the bad thing about motion is that it is so unpredictable." The motion concepts of cutting, screening, driving, and posting are more easily applied to different defensive looks, so even though every defensive look requires some adjustments, there are fewer offensive sets to learn. More precise decisions need to be made more often. Higher basketball IQ is also preferred. At practice, 3-on-3 and 4-on-4 work are valuable for all offensive teams but especially for motion teams. Players will learn that decisions are not made in a second, but in fractions of seconds. The windows close rapidly. Some players will try to use a lost advantage instead of moving on to the next read. Motion offense allows a team to design actions around specific player strengths.

 REFLECTION

TOM McCORMACK

We called this drill *Hunting for Shots*. There are times when shooting the ball is detrimental to the execution of half-court offense. However, since no points are awarded for execution, it is also important to recognize great shots. When running any type of half-court offense, players must understand that ball reversal where the ball hits three or four sides of the floor, making the extra pass, and creating post touches are crucial.

At times we rehearsed our offense in live 5-on-5 with those aforementioned concepts present. Initially, no shots were attempted, but each individual player, when in possession of the ball and open in a scoring area, had to recognize an open shot with a hard shot fake and yell "Shot!" The goal was shot recognition, so we counted the number of good shot recognitions without shooting rather than just try to run an offense without looking for a shot. We timed some possessions only looking for shot recognition without the actual shot.

The defense was determined to deny any clean looks at the basket. Not only did the defense deny the shot, it also tried to limit or pester the shot fake. This makes a big difference in intensity on both offense and defense and in the team and individual mindsets. If and when the offense achieved the established goal(s), we ended by allowing the offense to score. Because of the habits this type of execution instills, the offense continued to hunt for a great shot for whatever length of time it took. A great by product of the Hunt is the reinforcement of great shot fakes.

Checklist for Offense Preparation

- Transition offense: calls, numbers, and responsibilities
- M2M half-court offense
- Zone half-court offense
- Free throw situations and huddle
- Offensive free throw situations and huddle

    ~Special play

    ~Intentional miss situations

    ~Subbing to press after a make

- M2M special plays
- Zone special plays
- Delay

    ~vs. man defense/traps/zone

- Inbounds under

    ~vs. man defense

    ~vs. zone defense

- Press attack
- Last shot-clock situations

Models for Practice

If a buddy system is in place for morning practices, varsity practice starts the night before practice with the buddy partners checking with each other so that transportation to practice, pre-practice time start, notebooks, and practice uniforms were all in place. A possible team standard for pre-practice was a Marine quote, "If you're not early, you're late." All players were required to wear the team practice shorts, practice reversible, and team T-shirt, and bring a water bottle.

Buddies checked in upon arrival with each other and a designated coach. That responsibility is good for an assistant coach, especially an inexperienced one. The practice plan for the day is posted in the locker room and in the gym for the players to study during the pre-practice period before the official start of practice.

Pre-practice began with everyone on the practice floor ten minutes before the official practice start. Players work on stationary ballhandling and shooting form mechanics. Pre-practice ends with a quick jog to a brief team meeting at center court.

Time allowances for each segment were dependent on time of season, scouting, etc.

Both of us required that all players at each level tucked in their reversible jerseys for practice. It became one of the parts of our culture, to the point where the players reminded one another. Once established, the coaches rarely had to remind anyone. There were two reasons. First, jerseys are required to be tucked in during games. Second, and more importantly, it was the attention to detail about the little things that led to building a culture of attentiveness. Important enough that we have dedicated a whole chapter to attentiveness later in this book.

A Sample Progression for Practice:

- Static to dynamic stretch with a different partner every practice and static to dynamic warm-up or jump rope (completed in approximately 12 minutes)

- Sprint to a team meeting at mid-court to review practice plan. Then practice divides into segments usually done every day:

- Individual defensive work

- Individual offensive work

- Group defensive drills

- Group offensive drills

- Team defense-team offense

- Scrimmage-Always use the clock

- End-of game/clock special situations with focus shifting from offense to defense

- Sprint to a team meeting at mid-court to end practice

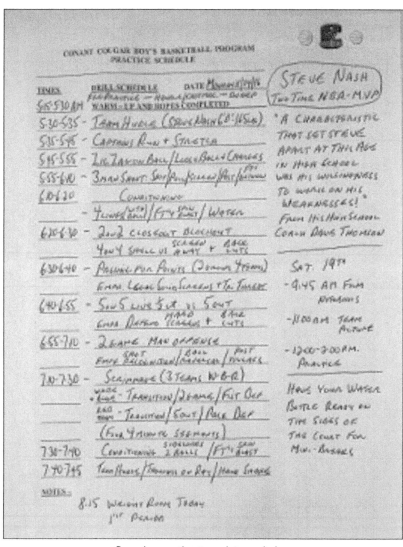

Sample practice template and plan

G. GENERATE FLOW CHARTS

FRESHMEN
Assume they know nothing. You're correct.

- Primary focus is classroom attitude and grades.

- Basketball focus is development. Winning is a goal, but secondary.

- Learn what playing hard means.

- Learn what being a teammate means.

- Start notebooks. Use them with monthly evaluations.

- Players learn what "good shape" means. Weight training should be instructed through form and technique.

- BALANCE AND FOOTWORK: starting and stopping, pivots, jab step and shot fake in a good triple threat

- DRIBBLING: saving the dribble, change of pace, off-hand, dribbles that create intelligent options, pull back-crossover, stutter. Maxim: Don't use the dribble until you have to. Once you start it, don't lose it until you have to.

- SHOOTING: correct form, off pass, off dribbles, off foot fakes and shot fakes. In addition, instruct shot from the catch off a screen away from the ball. Define for players what a "good shot" means.

- PASSING: post feeds, ball reversal options, fast break, pass fakes, full court passes. Avoid staring a hole into a potential receiver; keep eyes on the rim. Maxim: In order to be a threat to pass, you must be a threat to score.

- OFFENSE: "Take up court space" (Majerus). Man-to-man system with correct screening, acceptance of screens, hard cuts/Zone offense with use of dribble, pass fakes, inside-out spacing

- DEFENSE: "Take court space away" (Majerus). Man-to-man with stopping ball and penetration, help positions, gap positions, blocking out, use of the voice, correct rotations, charges and strips, transition, closeouts, loose ball reaction

- Which player can be elevated at mid-season from the "B" team to the "A" team, or moved from "A" to "B"? Who is most coachable? Who improves the most? Be aware of shoe sizes.

J-V/SOPHOMORES

They are now aware they knew nothing as
freshmen and want to know lots more.

- Primary focus is their classroom attitude and grades.
- Basketball focus is on continuous development with some winning.
- Balance and footwork polished with emphasis on foot and/or ball fakes to start offensive moves
- Continuation of notebooks with at least bi-weekly evaluations and conferences
- Continuation of learning to be a good teammate
- Doing everything better and quicker than last year with emphasis on footwork and faking
- Players develop muscle tone and understand great shape better with weekly weight training.
- Players learn what game speed means in drills and practice habits.
- Settling into a position with an eye down the road: Is a point guard emerging?
- Understanding details in the game with greater depth and application
- Are leaders emerging?
- DRIBBLING: moves that create an advantage, the off-hand improves or becomes a strength, the pullback dribble is used with efficiency
- PASSING: emphasis on the correct pass on the spot when the player is open, not after

- OFFENSE: applying system's offense with greater efficiency, more patience receiving and setting screens, improved offensive rebounding and more physical play

- Players follow a game plan with increasing acumen. They understand and apply good shot selection as the season progresses.

- DEFENSE: anticipating on defense instead of reacting, changing defenses, greater use of voice, focus on deflections/steals and improving consecutive stops, correct closeouts, obsession about blocking out

- Occasional practice or scrimmage with the varsity

VARSITY

Some are still clueless;
a few know something; a few know plenty.

Sophomores learn. Juniors make a leap and do what is asked with varying degrees of success. Seniors do what is required to win and execute their roles.

- Relentless pursuit of the details in execution of fundamentals

- Classroom a priority with an eye toward college choice

- Clear leadership, on and off the court

- Being a good teammate is understood and practiced.

- Notebooks continued and polished.

- Excellent conditioning with consistent weight training

- Foot and eye faking to start offensive moves is a confident part of team play.

- Cerebral play…Good focus for practice done off the court (scouting, game plan, etc.)

- Drills are performed at a varsity game speed and determined by the stopwatch, the coach, and the particular goals.

- Some players become students of the game.

- Varsity players are models for the lower levels. Good character is part of the team's core and M.O.
- Team blend of offensive execution dependent on good shot selection, game plan application, role recognition, system of play, individual talents, and outstanding defense
- Who is college-ready?

H. HANDLE THE PARTS OF THE SEASON

Within these three segments are tryouts, the first two weeks, the first game to Christmas, a Christmas Tournament, January to the end of the regular season, and the state tournament.

The Early Season

This segment begins with the start of practice to the Christmas tournament and emphasizes conditioning, fundamental drill work, installation and some experimentation of old and new Xs and Os, review of summer emphases, some experimentation with the playing rotation, and teammates becoming comfortable with each other.

At Conant for twenty-nine years and for five years at York High School, early season practice was 5:15 a.m. During tryouts at Conant, players were required to wear the green light shirts they earned during the off-season. Players who didn't earn one needed to wear their P.E. shirt. In order to try out at either school, all players were to have turned in the paperwork required by the athletic department. In addition, a player/parent/coaches' pledge agreement needed to be signed by all parties in order to try out. No extensions were given for missed deadlines. A suggestion is to keep all rules and regulations clear and enforceable. It was always wise to discuss rules with the administration first. For example, if the state's minimum requirement for academic-athletic eligibility is a 2.0 G.P.A., and you decide as the head of the basketball program to make it a 2.5, that disparity needs to be discussed with the administration before you proceed to make it law for the basketball players. We had a team-parent meeting on the day, or a few days, after tryouts to review expectations, explain the pledge, pass out practice and game schedules, and answer questions. The briefer the meeting the better, but the non-negotiable points must be clarified. The entire practice and game calendars were distributed to the players and parents after tryouts and at the pre-season parent meeting.

We focused on conditioning in the early season and gradually let up as the season progressed. We did a lot of individual skill work, group drills, and conditioning during the first two weeks leading up to the first game with more installation and team time the second week. On the sixth day of practice, usually the first Saturday, we practiced in the morning, then had a controlled scrimmage without officials for about an hour in the afternoon. At the end of the second week on either Friday or Saturday, we held scrimmages with officials before the first game of the season. Players were in their uniforms. On this night we invited the parents and family members to attend and take pictures on the court before the scrimmage. This tradition became popular and fun for our players and their families.

Balancing the amount of individual, group, team installation, scrimmage, and conditioning amounts at practices can be a delicate chore. Watching film and communicating scouting reports are also important considerations. With an overabundance of individual and group time, team execution suffers. Too much team and scrimmage time and you risk putting the cart before the horse, with the fundamentals necessary for execution losing sharpness. Probably the biggest factor here is what type of talent, experience, and leadership is returning from the previous season. Generally, the less you have, the more individual and group time you need. The more experience you have, the more time you can spend on team and scrimmage time because you have more help coming from the experienced leaders. Early examination of the season in these three phases helps a coach plan practice more effectively and saves time for the coach during the season. Flexibility, though, remains an important asset.

The Mid-Season

This segment covers the Christmas tournament until the end of the regular season. The focus of the team starts to narrow with Xs & Os, the playing rotation, role definition and acceptance, player-driven positive leadership, and player ownership. A few new, but necessary things might be added, but this is a time to tighten down, rather than experiment. Typically, we cut practice time down at some point during this segment from two hours to about 1.5 hours, but that was dependent on the game schedule. Conditioning during this time of the season was accomplished through challenging drill work and scrimmages. The intensity had to be obvious or the players found themselves on that wonderful baseline once again for a few sprints. In addition to the aforementioned narrow focus, this segment of the season communicates to players that their shape and wind are always essential to develop and maintain. Weight training too was cut down, but still done with more reps instead of maximum weights.

One skill that needs work every day is shooting, no matter the time of season. Generally speaking, defense can be more consistent than offense, but field goal shooting and free throw shooting remain huge impacts on the momentum of games. Never ignore shooting.

The Late Season

This segment goes from mid-February through the state tournament and defines what all the previous segments have tried to accomplish. At this point teams want to be playing at the top of their game with offenses and defenses, the playing rotation, and player roles in place and humming. Some adjustments are made in game plans for certain opponents, but there is no experimentation. Once the tournament starts, practice time is limited, maybe only a walk-through or chalk talk. At this point in the season, being rested, prepared, and confident in the system and each other are the essentials.

A point to consider: Besides shortening practice time during the mid-season, there might be a time change for practice, if facilities and conditions allow. We changed from morning practice during the early and mid-segments to a 3:30 p.m. practice in the late season segment. The other winter sports are usually over by then, and we found that the change (just like changing up drills or conditioning at practice) is refreshing for the players and coaches at that time of the season. We ran a 3-point shooting contest with the players and coaches at the end of the mid-season segment. Coaches have plenty of options with any changes in practice routine, but the idea was to have some fun and then get down to business because reality had arrived: win and advance or lose and go home. We told our players that except for Sunday, they had little time for social life.

Players committed to focusing on schoolwork, resting, and preparing. Losing is hard to swallow at any time, but even harder without total preparation. We lived with this outcome: Give it everything we have both on and off the court, then let the chips fall where they may. Every detail, every skill, every meeting, and every practice had been planned and directed to expect VICTORY.

I. INTEGRATE "DEFENSE VS. OFFENSE"

"Offense wins games and defense wins championships."

In other words, offense can win some battles,
but it's defense that wins the war.

"Defense travels well."

On the road offense will have some off nights, but defense is constant.

*"Great offensive players are made from April through October,
but great defensive teams are made from November through March."*

The off-season, the day after the team plays its last game
in the state tournament, is the time for individuals to build
the Big 3 offensive skills, gain strength, and condition.
It is also a time for leaders to emerge.

Plenty of these sayings abound, some quite accurate. There are also numerous priorities about the various types of defensive and offensive philosophies. Part of the real beauty of the game is that there is more than one way to get the job done. These systems run the gamut from full court pressure, denial, and trapping to "pack line" man-to-man and various types of zones. The defense has as much or more to do with establishing the pace of play as does the offense. Regardless of the type of defense, Early, Loud, and Often are the vocal evaluators demanded by good coaches from their players during every defensive possession.

In games where the shot clock is in effect, many defenses have evolved to pushing the offense to attempt a contested shot against the shot clock. In fact, teams that can do this consistently and limit the offense to one shot are usually pretty successful. Having offensive players who can make plays has become a priority. Unfortunately, a lot of the players with these special scoring and assisting skills will force a shot or a tough pass rather than make the extra pass that leads to a great shot. The shot clock might as well disappear from view with some teams and players.

As we mentioned earlier, Dick Bennett believes that in the half court a team can do three things on defense: help, deny, and recover, but can only do two of them well. Likewise, we taught players that in half-court offense they can do three things: space, screen, and dribble drive, but can only do two of them well. The ball screen does try to facilitate spacing and dribble penetration but initially brings two players and the ball to the same spot.

We are not advocating any particular style of defense or offense, but as high school coaches, it was never much fun watching a team run up and down the floor (especially our own) with players who weren't good shooters/scorers. It has been our observation that if our team was going to push the pace, we better have players who can shoot and finish in transition, penetrate, make great decisions, or offensive rebound well. If coaches have all or some of those players, why should they slow the game down and limit possessions? If they don't and the other team does, why not limit the number of possessions? If recruiting is a non-factor, coaches will probably find themselves on both sides of the spectrum over the course of time. All those pieces fill in the puzzle of preparation.

If you have ever exchanged Xs and Os with another coach, you know the guy with the marker in his hand last always wins. Having said that, let's take a look at defense vs. offense with that perspective.

DEFENSE

If you are a pack line team, you must take away transition baskets first and foremost. Once it gets to 5-on-5 in the half court, the goals are no rhythm 3s, no penetration, no post up baskets, and no second shots.

OFFENSE

If you are attacking one of these, try to fastbreak before it becomes 5-on-5 or share and reverse the ball. Penetration will be difficult, so solid screening and ball reversal are better options. These defensive teams do not want to be put in long closeout situations or broken down from the four concepts they are built to eliminate. Patience is essential to beat this defense. Force nothing until an end of the quarter or shot clock situation dictates. Shooting a high percentage bodes well in your favor.

DEFENSE

Using switching screens or a matchup zone can create confusion and hesitation. These defenses can be effective if your players can guard multiple positions or skill sets. Vision and communication, always important, are now critical. These teams have a tendency to head turn and lose the ball at times.

OFFENSE

Be aware of the switcher jumping out in the passing lane; a bounce pass on the perimeter can especially be fatal. Pass fakes, back cut action, slip screens, and hard cutting action are moves to apply. Sometimes by screening his/her own defender, the screener can block off two defenders. Screening with a strong seal will initially have the new defender behind the screener, so a seal and role move can be effective. An ideal situation here is a big player setting a screen for a smaller teammate. New matchup situations are constantly being created so be aware of advantages both in the post and on the perimeter.

DEFENSE

Say you play 1-2-2 ¾-court, a 2-2-1 ¾ tempo press, or 1-2-2, 1-3-1, or 2-3 half-court zones. These defenses can be great equalizers if your team is overmatched. Those zones can slow the game down and create chaos with deflections and passing lane confusion. Conversely, these defenses can also keep a lesser team in the game longer if your team has a skill advantage. These types of defensive teams might play defense for longer periods and have less possession time than the opponent.

OFFENSE

Against any press a good progression of sight for the player with the ball is to look strong sideline, middle, diagonal, and reverse. These actions are done quickly. Eye and pass fakes will freeze defenders or get them out of position. We called our press offense "press attack," not "press break" because attack was our mindset. The best way to stop an opponent's use of a press is to score. Half court spacing is critical along with cuts and spot-ups from behind defenders who are staring at the ball. Some screening should be employed. The use of the dribble has to be emphasized to create disadvantages. Players have to drive into gaps. Use of the pull-back dribble is necessary if the gaps close quickly. Zone teams have a more difficult time boxing out, so offensive rebounding becomes a key part of the attack.

Pass faking, penetrating to draw two defenders, and making a defender guard two passes are also excellent against zones. Another suggestion: if you use a mobile big player to break pressure over half-court, have that player catch, pivot, pass to either wing and dive into the post after the pass. That simple move can be very effective and hard to guard for the defense which is settling back into its half-court defense.

DEFENSE

Using a 1-2-1-1 full-court press, a man-to-man faceguard press, or a run and jump trapping press back to a pressure and denial, or a trapping ½-court defense will increase the pace of the game. Creating tempo, multiple possessions, open floor space, and disruptions of the offense with deflections, turnovers, and rushed shots are the goals for these pressing defenses.

OFFENSE

On the press attack, getting the ball inbounds and the outlet pass from a defensive rebound or turnover initially requires good floor spacing. Players must know how to get to the open spot. Then the same progression follows looking up the floor as the other presses. These defenses will be scrambling a lot, so good spacing in the gaps with pass and eye fakes will open up appropriate attacking, scoring, ball reversal, and pressure release opportunities. The same is true for attacking the half-court trapping defense. A high post or 3-point line pressure release is also a help here, especially if the release is a bigger player who can pass and shoot. Pass fakes and back cuts are particularly useful against teams that use those pressures.

DEFENSE

If you are a team that changes defenses, the offense is forced to recognize the exact defense and attack it appropriately. This can lead to indecision and hesitation by the offense, a big advantage for the defense. We sometimes used this defensive strategy depending on whether we scored or not. There are several different timings, combinations of defense, and signal strategies a team can apply: time outs, free throw situations, or substitutions. A word of caution here. Will your team become a "jack of all trades and master of none"? The team might get very good at changing defenses but might not be able to master any of them. When you have to have the ball, what is your team's best defense?

OFFENSE

What is your main theory of offense here? Do you teach and coach offense by learning continuity patterns and plays, or do you coach basic principles of offense that your team can apply to almost any defensive look? A big decision. If it is the first type, your team must recognize the defense and attack with the specific offense. Some teams are very good at running specific patterns against specific defensive looks. This requires extensive team time on offense at practice and a good point guard. Some of these sets are drastically different in execution. That time will take away from precious shooting and skill work. Obviously, some adjustments need to be made depending on the situation but playing with basic offensive motion principles against any defense will limit the number of changes for what the other team dictates. Make sure the players who need the ball in scoring, assisting, and rebounding situations are getting it. No matter which type you prefer, those are the basic questions to ask about any offensive set. Don't run a pattern just to run the pattern. Many teams run beautifully coordinated offenses that don't get the ball to the necessary player. Coaches, we know we ask this question throughout this book, but it is paramount to intelligent preparation: "Should the system fit the players or players fit the system?" Teams that have answered the other questions and understand the why tend to have great player-coaches on the floor. They may be beaten, but they don't lose.

DEFENSE

Periodically playing a box +1, triangle+2, or some gimmick defense can disrupt an offense. One of these defenses may even be a changing defense within that coach's philosophy. Outmanned teams or teams facing one or two great scorers will sometimes use this strategy to limit these players' touches or to attempt to level the playing field. Some teams might switch to it during the game to take away a hot hand or to create a momentum swing. This defense relies on surprise. It might be the case where the opponent has not practiced against it much or has yet to see it in a game.

OFFENSE

As the coach, if you desire to prepare your team well, you will show your team those defenses, especially if you have one or two primary scorers. You should do so early in the season; in this way, players get a complete picture. These gimmick defenses are rarely a team's primary defense, and even if a certain one is, there are holes in it. Rather than offer specifics, we ask you the basic questions of who, where, how, how often, and when. Then design and practice it maybe once a week. We almost always review it for an opponent we had beaten once already and for everyone in the state tournament. Similar to the last section on playing and attacking changing defenses, the offense against these defenses does not have to be drastically different.

More Defensive and Offensive Ideas

DEFENSE

Never neglect inbounds defense, especially under the defensive basket. Scouting will influence this area. Do you switch men, fight through, go zone, put a man on the ball, or see the ball and the man?

OFFENSE

What is the signal to start the play? Most use the slap of the ball by the inbounder. We started on the handoff from the referee because some defenses are not ready for this. Is your philosophy just to safely inbound the ball or to create a score? We had a safety valve on the sideline as a failsafe outlet. The inbounder counted to three and if the scoring option was not open, the safety valve received the pass. We rarely turned the ball over and if we did, the ball sailed out of bounds, so it could not be converted to points by the other team on a steal. How many times in any level of basketball do you see a ball lobbed all the way past half-court on a baseline out of bounds play? This pass is not only risky, but it also suggests a lack of preparation and attention to details.

DEFENSE

Continually practice ball, gap, and help responsibilities no matter what defense you play. These concepts apply to all defenses with specific rules in place dependent on the defense or the opponent. The possession is not over until your team secures the ball on a defensive rebound or turnover. Finish the possession.

OFFENSE

Who are your scorers? How are they being defended? How many true scorers do you have? Knowing these answers gives you the feedback needed to prioritize spacing, movement, and screening. Keep in mind that ball reversal can really break a defense down and backscreens are a shooter's best friend. Scorers must learn to move intelligently without the ball by using changes of speed and direction to get free. Rick Majerus told scorers that with their intelligent movement, the ball will find them. The smart offensive player determines when the race starts. You might also consider looking at the other side of the coin: If you were planning to defend your own team's best scorers, what would you do?

DEFENSE

What are your favorite defensive rebounding drills? These should be wars, a term Michigan State University head coach Tom Izzo loves. In this context, the NBA stands for "No Babies Allowed." Coach Hubie Brown said, "Teams and players that attack a defensive rebounder are a sign of a young and inexperienced team." Some teams unknowingly do this and don't correct it which results in giving up easy baskets or committing unnecessary fouls. A power out dribble and outlet pass are lethal weapons when teams attack or trap the rebounder.

OFFENSE

What are your favorite offensive rebounding drills? The shot is the first part of the possible conversion to defense. How many players do you send to the offensive glass? We sprinted three players to specific spots to form an offensive rebounding triangle covering both sides and the front of the rim and the other two players back to the top of the key and half-court on the release of the shot for defensive coverage. Having at least one player back on defense on the shot attempt is paramount to stopping an opponent's break. There are more concepts and drills in the Rebounding chapter.

Defense and Offense in Special Situations

Free Throw Situations

Five players sprinted to huddle on free throws to the volleyball line in the lane on defense and to the free throw line on offense. Sprint there, quick look to coach, communicate what's next, and hustle to the practiced spot. If we were on defense, we always had our two players closest to the shooter switch spots across the lane on a two and on a three-shot foul after each attempt to try to throw off the shooter's rhythm.

Jump Ball Situations

Getting the jump ball in an overtime can be critical, so work on winning or stealing it. Spots and responsibilities on the jump ball should be practiced. If the opponent scores on the jump ball, your scouting and preparation are suspect. Just like free throws situations with players on the lane, we wanted players bending their knees and keeping the hands higher than the opponent's arms.

Side Inbounds

This is not as lethal as under the basket. Two important questions are: How do you play the post, and do you put a defender on the ball?

End of Clock and Game Situations

Last shot defense and offense was one of our last parts of preparation for every opponent. Time, score, bonus situation, and possession arrow are critical points. Examples of defenses we practiced: guard the arc, switch all screens, give no help and stay attached to shooters, foul to stop the clock, and know who to foul. We also had a few essential plays based on score and time. We desired our last-second shot to be attempted with five or six seconds left on the clock. If we missed, there was a chance for an offensive rebound or tip-in. We never ignored these situations the day before a game and in any pre-practice the day of the game.

Walk throughs and/or shoot arounds before a game varied with previous practice time and travel time but should also be planned well. Never give players the impression that a pre-game shootaround or walk-through is a time to divert from sound practice habits. Scouting report and game plan review time should put the finishing touch on preparation for an opponent.

J. JUICE UP FOR GAMES

Obviously, coaches want their players to execute a game plan as well as possible, then see the result on the scoreboard. Human nature being what it is-and not to forget we are dealing with teenagers-execution of a game plan to a coach's complete delight is a rarity, even in victory. There is so much out of both coaches' and players' control during the course of games even though coaches do everything they can to prepare their teams in all aspects. These unpredictable factors make the game both fun and nerve racking. If prepared, everyone does the best they can do in the moment.

REFLECTION

TOM ANSTETT

I planned and wrote an index card that had keys to the game and offenses and defenses pertinent to that opponent. I kept that card in my shirt pocket. It was a quick review I used at key points in the game. I also developed the habit before a game but after the team left the locker room for its warm-up to look into a mirror and tell myself that tonight there will be one person in the stands who has never seen me coach. I wanted that person to leave the gym knowing that my team was well coached and competitive, no matter the outcome.

Game Prep

"We wanted to be playing chess while the other team was playing checkers." That statement by former University of Wisconsin basketball coach Bo Ryan epitomizes the cumulative efforts of all great coaches when determining the desired mental advantage during the actual game. Ryan was talking specifically about his half-court offense against any opponent's man-to-man defense. That being said, all coaches want to have the feeling before a game-and during it-that they will outcoach their rivals on the other bench. The chess player knows strategy, anticipates moves from the opponent, is mentally tough, thirsts for the competition, and assumes nothing. What a disturbing feeling for a coach who has a prolific scorer yet does not prepare the team or that one player for a box and one defense, thinking that there is no way the upcoming opponent will use that defense. After all, it was never used once during the season. Leave no stone unturned.

Game Management

Having a "feel for the flow of the game" is a talent some coaches have more than others. That feel is an intrinsic one, a move in the gut that tells a coach what to do, who to sub, when to call a timeout, how to react, etc. Experience and knowledge of personnel teach coaches this feel.

The list below contains factors for game management. Each one needs consideration and planning.

- Pre-game: uniform and gear check, locker room deadline, pre-game meeting deadline, food deadline

- Warm-up

- Bench organization and expectations

- Assistants' responsibilities

- Player responsibilities

- Managers' responsibilities…Hope you have a couple good ones. Good ones are invaluable.

- Video responsibilities

- Statistics

- Substitution routine

- Time out organization (full and 30 seconds)

- Referees/technical fouls/sportsmanship expectations

- Scorekeeper responsibilities

- First quarter and first few possessions, surprises

- Second quarter and last two minutes

- Halftime: organization, adjustments, responsibilities, momentum swings

- Third quarter and first two minutes

- Fourth quarter: time and score, bonus situation for both teams, last 4-minute finishers, key specials on offense/defense/personnel, possession arrow

- Overtime: same as the fourth quarter plus the jump ball

- Leaving the bench and floor after the game
- Post-game talk and locker room procedures and expectation
- Talking to the press
- Dismissal routine and expectations for that night and the next day

Post-Game

After a tough loss, say as little as possible. Players are not paying as close attention as you might want or think. After a big win, raise the roof about both mistakes and good efforts. Players are tuned in, excited, and motivated. Engage those energies. The late Al McGuire, Marquette University coach from 1964-1977 and the first coach to be ejected from a national championship game, noted as much when he stated, "After a loss, shut up. After a win, talk as much as you want."

Post-game emotions by coaches are deceiving. Coaches can think that their teams played lousy, but after watching the game, see that the effort wasn't as bad as they thought. Or vice versa. Film does not lie or distort the truth, so it is prudent to temper emotions after the game, so that the foot does not have to come out of the mouth later. In addition, any one player and/or the entire team will accept criticism or praise better if given the opportunity to see the actual sequence. Keep in mind, what you say might not be what players hear and take home to inquisitive parents.

"The test of our progress is not whether we add more
to the abundance of those who have much;
it is whether we provide enough for those who have little."

~Franklin Roosevelt

R – RESILIENCE

"This game honors toughness."

~Brad Stevens
Boston Celtics Coach

"There is a lot of basketball beyond our control,
but a player should never let anyone try harder than he does."

~(the late) Dean Smith
University of North Carolina

"Sweet are the uses of adversity."

~Shakespeare
As You Like It (1599) Act 2, sc. 1, l. 12

POINTS TO PONDER

- Resilience is essential. One cannot win without resilience.

- Teams have to be just as resilient after victories as they are after defeats.

- A game's peaks and valleys test the resilience of the players and the coach.

- Who says you cannot teach resilience? Model it. Preach it. Make it a theme for the year. Connect it to real life situations. There are few limits to this instruction. Witness: Coach Tony Bennett took over at the University of Virginia in 2009, vowing to build "a program that lasts." In 2015 his team started 19-0, but a key injury was one of the factors that led to a second-round defeat at the hands of Michigan State. In 2018 Bennett's top seed lost a first-round shocker to the 16th seed, UMBC. Despite the unending criticism, that program was one "to last." The following year Bennett's Cavaliers beat Texas Tech to win the national championship. ESPN called Virginia's 2018–19 campaign "the most redemptive season in the history of college basketball."

- Taking the charge on defense is one of the best examples of resilience. In his senior year at Lincoln-Way East High School in Frankfort, Illinois, John Anstett took 33 charges. It's possible.

- The late Gordon Gillespie, the renowned football coach at Joliet Catholic High School and baseball coach at the University of St. Francis in Joliet, Illinois, spoke to summer camps with this message, "Anyone who plays athletics takes risks of injury, disappointment, frustration, or fleeting glory; but the gains outweigh the risks." Each of those stages constitute a level of resilience a player will face.

- Very few teams finish a season undefeated. In the NCAA Division-I tournament, there have only been seven undefeated teams, the last one being Indiana University in 1975-76.

How does resilience reveal itself in a basketball program? What evidence can a coach see for the growth of resilience in his/her players?

- One has to acknowledge and praise the effort and resilience of the freshman B-team player who endures and evolves from the last player on the B team to a starter and/or contributor on the varsity. We have known such young people, those freshmen who lacked skills, muscle, or confidence, yet refused to allow their dreams or desire to vanish. We have witnessed that one player, who was the last one to make the team at age 14, develop into a reliable, tough player due to four years of grit, practice, and perseverance. Those particular players are prime reasons why we coach. Coaches end up praising them as seniors at their awards nights. Long after they have graduated, their presence and example renew through those freshmen who follow.

- In his book The Winner Within, Pat Riley states, "Strive for excellence, not perfection." That particular frame of mind separates those players who overcome the odds and bounce back quickly from setbacks. Those players stay in the moment, pushing for their goals with unselfishness and toughness.

- Resilient people and players avoid comparisons; they focus on their own development in unselfish ways.

- The self-talk of the resilient is powerful, steady, and optimistic. I Can and I Will are personal vows and belief systems.

- Every player improves throughout a season. The more resilient ones improve more and take responsibility for their own improvement. They are eager to learn every day. Michael Jordan stated, "I have missed more than 9,000 shots in my career. I have lost almost 300 games. On 26 occasions I have been entrusted to take the game winning shot, and I missed. I have failed over and over and over again in my life. And that is why I succeed."

- There is little whining or blaming within the sphere of resilience.

- When needed, your resilient defenders will get a 5-second call on the opponent's attempted inbound pass.

- Your team outrebounds a bigger opponent.

- Your players get up quicker than they fall down.

- Your players rally from a large deficit to win after the best player fouls out.

- Your team blows a big lead, but rebounds to win with clutch plays.

- Your team responds with a great week of practice and a gut-check Friday victory the week after a heartbreaking loss.

- Your injured player returns to play much earlier than the doctor's predictions.

 REFLECTION

TOM ANSTETT

My son T.J. incurred a serious injury in both his sophomore and junior years. A stress fracture in his back and then a badly sprained ankle kept him out of action for what amounted to an entire season. He never hung his head and worked diligently after each injury to get back as soon as he could. I admired him for that resilience.

- Your players continue to beat the stopwatch and beat their times in wind sprints.

- Your players hold their heads up and meet your eyes with theirs after a tough loss.

- Your players respect officials, no matter the coach's and/or fans' reactions or the believability of a call.

- Your players play with a next play mentality. This belief manifests positive and enthusiastic body language, spoken language, and poise.

- Your players play outstanding defense every game, no exception.

- Resilient players do not showboat because they immediately focus on the next play. One example is a player making a 3-point shot and then drawing attention by pointing to the crowd or making some gesture, instead of sprinting back on defense, getting in stance, and converting to a disposition to dominate the offense. In other words, they do not mimic many NBA players.

- .300 hitters in baseball and 40% 3-point shooters in basketball are considered to be performing that skill at a high level in those respective sports. However, they are dealing with failure more than half the time. If you have never failed, you have never really tried. (Anonymous)

- When taken with the right perspective, losses can help a team improve just as much as winning. Winning can mask deficiencies. Losing exposes deficiencies.

REFLECTION

TOM ANSTETT

My father Carl modeled resilience. He co-owned a tool and die shop for over 40 years with his brother. Every day he rose around 5 a.m. to drive to his work. He could fix just about anything, a trait I never inherited. In my youth, he worked on some Saturdays too, but typically only five days a week, 10-12 hours a day. He and my uncle shared the shop with my dad responsible for all the physical aspects: setting up presses, organizing the labor, repairing broken machines and tools, and teaching employees the necessary routines or methods for production. My uncle Jim took care of all the paperwork relevant to a business: invoices, applications, and payroll. After working all day with the hovering pressures of ownership pushing him to achieve a living for his family, he walked into our bungalow on the northwest side of Chicago, smiled, and kissed my mother. We sat together for suppers. My dad was never too tired to bypass playing catch in the back alley with me. We donned the baseball gloves, grabbed a baseball, and threw the ball for thirty minutes. This catch became a nightly ritual, just me and Dad. Talk about resilience; he never let the peaks and valleys of the day interfere with spending some valuable time with his son. Furthermore, he could pitch with either arm. His righty throws had the speed; the lefty possessed the craftiness with the knuckleball and the sinker. He never seemed to have a bad day.

In my teenage years when I was playing high school basketball at Quigley Seminary-North, his many examples of resilience resounded in my own play. In one game in my junior year, I was being manhandled under the boards. When we talked after the game, all he said was, "You never give up no matter what is happening. Always get after the ball. You'll learn." In another instance in my senior year, after I had enjoyed a particularly good game and victory, he said, "What matters is if you string good games together with no letup, no matter the outcomes." His words were few, but their effects tremendous. In some of those brief encounters in many long, rigorous practices under Coach Schaefer, and in some of the toughest games, I recalled his work ethic, toughness, and resilience. Those traits carried me then and do now. I see them also in my sons.

Andy Laux was an outstanding player at Immaculate Conception High School from 1980-1984. Heady and competitive, he was my point guard at 6'5" and had a knack for making the right play at the right time. He received a full basketball scholarship to DePaul University when Joey Meyer was the head coach, but not without earning it. Meyer had reservations about Andy. Was he quick enough? Athletic enough? Emotionally tough enough for Division-I basketball? In the moment Meyer was sold, he and assistant coach Jim Molinari sat a couple of rows behind our bench. Molinari was very enthused about Andy and had followed him all season, so he brought Coach Meyer for a final look. In the first game of our regional-state tournament, a tournament where we were favored to make it downstate after a 24-win regular season, Andy began the game with turnovers and sluggish play. We were losing early to a team we had beaten twice in the regular season and looking bad. I took Andy out after the first six minutes-not a normal occurrence. When one of our players was subbed, that player had to sit next to me until I was finished speaking to him. After watching Andy play those six minutes, I screamed at him about his carelessness and lack of energy. I rarely yelled at Andy; he was our leader and his play poised and consistent all year. However, in that instance, he heard it all. His eyes never left my wrath. He immediately began encouraging his teammates, even coaching them from the sidelines. There was no pouting, no resistance, no backtalk, no head down. He knew he had to energize himself, and he did so by supporting his team. He never left my side. I put him back into the game in the second quarter. The reliable, confident Andy emerged from that point: scoring when needed, making timely decisions with the ball, leading his team to a 15-point win. That moment did not happen by accident. It was the result of endless training and resilience on Andy's part.

After the game, Meyer was convinced. As he said to me later, "Tom, when you took him to task after you took him out, that was all I needed to see. We want him; his basketball sense is exceptional, and he is so unselfish. He took your correction like a man. Molinari had him pegged correctly all along, but I had to see for myself." Meyer's final look was a testimony to in-person scouting, too.

With the help of exceptional parents, Andy learned resilience. He practices it today as a fine social studies teacher at Hinsdale Central High School in Hinsdale, Illinois.

Resilience is one of the most essential life lessons that basketball, or any sport, teaches. No athletes have everything go their own way to a comfortable level throughout an entire season. Resilience also goes well beyond basketball, of course, since the context in any situation varies for the amount of resilience necessary. I believe every athlete should read Unbroken by Laura Hillenbrand. This nonfiction tells the story of Olympic hero Louis Zamperini, a World War II pilot whose plane crashes in the Pacific in 1943. After 47 days at sea, he is captured by the Japanese and held in various POW camps until the end of the war. In those camps he and his fellow prisoners were brutally tortured and mistreated, with Zamperini singled out most often for punishments. Yet he persevered. His story is one any athlete will appreciate.

 REFLECTION

TOM McCORMACK

Show Up and Team Up. Those two maxims reflect my parents, Emmett and Joan, and two of the many gifts they bestowed on me. Within both of those treasures, resilience was its silent partner.

Dad worked 44 years at the Merchandise Mart in Chicago as an elevator operator and starter without missing one day. Dad was a high school basketball player and Mom a swimmer/diver and city champion tennis player. Because of my mother, I never missed a day of school from third grade through high school. "Aw, come on Mom. I don't feel good," versus, "Get up; you're fine. You're going," was our morning, one-way conversation on more than one occasion.

Fortunately, my parents valued education and sports: education as a time-honored way to improve life, and sports as a vehicle to balance and supplement that education. From the time I was in Little League and played on the fifth-grade basketball team at St. Genevieve School on the northwest side of Chicago, through college and after, my parents made it to almost every game I played. Mom was our head Little League baseball coach for one season when the original coach had to drop out. None of the dads volunteered, so Mom took over. To her and Dad, it didn't matter what position I played or my amount of playing time; thus, initial lessons in resilience arrived early. When I was twelve, I was in my last year of Little League. Both my team, the Braves, and I were having a great year. I had just been told that I had made the all-star team for the post-season tournament that eventually led the winning teams to Williamsport, Pennsylvania, the mecca for Little League players. Toward the end of the season, I was in a bicycle accident. I tore a ligament in my knee which ended my season. Deep depression. My season was over, or so I thought. I was in a brace on Wednesday and that Friday our team had a game. I remember sitting around the house feeling sorry for myself. My mom came into my room and said, "Come on. It's time to get to the field for pre-game practice." Since I couldn't play, I did not want to go, but they had other ideas. While in the car, they talked to me about the importance of being present to support my teammates. Mom told me, "Now when you get to the field, you ask Coach Wolski what you can do to help him and the team." I really didn't want to, but I knew arguing was fruitless. Coach assigned me to coach first base which became my job for the rest of the season. He gave me some responsibility, and I took it seriously. I got my first experience coaching at twelve years old and even though I didn't realize it at the time, got one of the best lessons of my life. My parents showed up for every game then, too.

They teamed up to support my resilience and dedication to my basketball career, no matter how they felt or what the day. They came to most of the games I coached during the regular seasons from 1984 through 2014. They attended many spring and summer league games, too. Mom even kept her own game and team statistics, in between reminding the referees of their errors in judgement. At the end of my first two seasons as head coach at Conant High School, we were a combined 2-48. Dealing with that challenge required some serious lessons in resiliency. I had an idea of what I was getting into when I took the job. The program had won a total of 11 games in the previous five seasons. Mom and Dad were there for every one of those 50 games the first two years. They and my wife Mary never let me down during those years. It was great having them there in the third year to enjoy the first of many winning seasons. However, having them there during those 48 losses was their most valuable example of resilience.

People noticed my parents' visibility. In 1994 Mom and Dad were inducted into the Illinois Basketball Coaches Hall of Fame in the "Friends of Basketball" category. Ed Molitor, a terrific coach and H.O.F. member, nominated my parents after getting to know them and commenting, "They are at everything."

My parents showed me that the most precious gift people can give others is the gift of time. Quality over quantity. Quality time promotes a focus and a toughness. A sport's physical skills are one thing, but the lessons learned along the way, such as teamwork and resilience are the long-lasting results. What was important was that we showed up, gave it our best shot, and then did it all over again. That outlook allowed me to stay in coaching for as long as I have. In the spring of 2020, I finished my 50th consecutive year coaching at various levels, with 33 as a high school head coach. Moreover, my wife Mary and I will soon celebrate our 44th wedding anniversary. We have raised four great children. Proud about those accomplishments in my life, I know that resilience plays a major role in accomplishing anything worthwhile. Show Up and Team Up remain the cornerstones of our marriage and family.

Right after school ended in early June, we ran a summer camp for all of our levels, incoming freshmen, sophomores, and varsity. For some of the sessions, all of the levels were together. I had the entire group sit together at one of these sessions and asked the freshman, "Why are you here?" The most frequent answer was to get better. I then explained, "While you certainly should improve some while at camp, the biggest lesson you should learn is determining how to improve. The skills and drills done at camp are a mere fraction of the time needed. You need to do them on your own and make them your own to really improve. The skills and drills we cover in camp are those you need to work on. Realistically, after any basketball camp, your confidence and skill levels may slip some because you are trying to incorporate what is being taught. None of it is muscle-memory or instinctive. Doing the skills correctly over the course of time breeds better skill and confidence."

I then asked all the freshman present to stand and look around. There might be as many as fifty or more. Everyone took notice. I had them sit down, and then asked the sophomores, then the juniors to do the same thing. Finally, I asked the seniors to stand. Each group was considerably smaller than the previous one. The senior group usually numbered about seven, give or take one or two.

I then explained that this being only June with tryouts in early November, the senior number would be even smaller by then. Coming to this camp is the easy part. Getting to the point where the seniors are in November will take a lot of work away from here. Doing other sports is okay, and you can make that challenge work because quality of time is more important than quantity. Establishing priorities and time management skills are big parts of the next step towards goal achievement. The higher skill levels in basketball take a lot of quality time to perfect, so they come at a cost. There are no shortcuts. There are no promises that you will get the role you want or even a spot on the team. I then told the freshmen that when these standing seniors were freshman like they are, they had as many in their freshman group as you do now. Most of the ones who were no longer in the program were not cut. They decided the commitment to the offseason work was not a priority.

Usually, at least a couple in the group of seniors were B-team players as freshmen or maybe someone who was cut as a freshman. The point I was trying to hammer home was that the decision, if they are still present and standing when they are seniors, has a lot more to do with their individual level of commitment than the coach's decision. Most players have survived some practices or workouts that were not fun. Probably the most common thing kids say if they quit is, "It's not fun." What they really mean is, "I don't want to commit to do what it takes to be a part of the program." Not seeing themselves getting the role they want also was another default.

Somewhere along the line, whether it's fun or not, the players who hang in there learn to embrace the work. Embracing is a true level of mental and physical achievement, a level that includes fun. They understand that there is no guarantee at the end and that the real reward is the process. Strengths become stronger and weaknesses become strengths. No matter what the role, a player who makes it through senior year becomes a master of resilience. Within that big investment comes the well-deserved pride of ownership.

Having been a high school head coach for 33 years, I run into a lot of former players: those who finished in the program as seniors and those who left sometime before their senior year. 100% of the finishers are proud of their accomplishment and tell me I'm too soft on the current players. Likewise, the next player I come across who left the program on his own before finishing and says he does not regret the decision will be the first one.

"Don't give up; don't ever give up."

~Jim Valvano

0 – OFF-SEASON

"Think training's hard? Try losing."
~(Nike Motivation)

"When I think about the playoffs, my nipples get hard."
~Enes Kanter

"Dedication is more important than ability."
~(the late) Bob Richards
Olympic Champion

"The season belongs to the coach. The off-season belongs to the players."
~Pat Sullivan
University of St. Francis

POINTS TO PONDER

A series of thoughts about off-season preparation follows. You will discover an entire plan of collective energy and individual workouts. All of this information guides our belief that spring and summer preparation focuses on players' individual development; team progress is useful, but secondary. We also believe that an excess of 5-on-5 is counterproductive to individual development. Some might say that having a team learn new offenses and plays has to be primary, but we feel that if players develop more strength, more offensive skills based on their ability and position, read about the game, work out as an individual or with a teammate, play more 1-on-1 and 3-on-3 than 5-on-5, that those players will develop much more confidence. So too will a team's offense thrive even more in the regular season.

A word about AAU, an organization that has enveloped, sometimes smothered, individual development. AAU can be helpful. Helpful, not the be-all and end-all for improvement, as it is often seen today. Players will experience more competition, sometimes good, and gain some exposure, but often the team concept and practices are based upon lots of 1-on-1 with dribble overkill, not to mention a lack of fundamentals. Sometimes the worst job on an AAU team is inbounding the ball after the opponent scores; that same player might not see the ball again on subsequent possessions. A healthy abundance of 3-on-3 and 1-on-1 ensures that players have the ball in their hands and learn to move without the ball with greater efficiency. Whatever players decide to do, it is essential that they play hard with goal-driven and aggressive play. They will have good days and rough ones, but every time they have a ball in their hands, they have the opportunity to improve. Also, we believe it is far better to work with maximum effort and enthusiasm for 1 to 1.5 hours, then spend three hours "shooting around" (See the Four Levels of Preparation at the end of this section.). Working out without specific goals or planning wastes time, and time, as is said in folklore, "Waits for no one."

The term "open gym" is just that…open to interpretation and attendance. Open gyms are open to the entire school, so who shows up is anyone's guess. Guiding players to constructive workouts during open gyms is a challenge for coaches. Leadership from the seniors and the better players is instrumental for open gyms to be productive and contributing to the progress of the program. One suggestion: If possible, run the open gyms in the mornings before school begins. See who shows up then. No matter if it's open gym or camps, in season or out of season, much of the activity is voluntary. No one forces a player to play sports. Players should not send a messenger when they are unable to attend; instead they should call or see the coach in person during the day to explain the absence. The communication is more important than the reason.

TIPS FOR A MORE PRODUCTIVE OFF-SEASON
Think and Talk About the Game
We encourage players to arrive at spring and summer league games a little early or stay a little late and watch other teams play to analyze what those teams are doing on offense and defense. What's different from the way we do things?

For example, why do they play offense that way? Watch individual players and figure out their strengths and weaknesses. Watch your teammates at camp and open gym. Analyze their play. Encourage them to do the same. These observations will be even more valuable when teammates and coaches talk with one another. There is a tremendous amount of knowledge among us. We have built many successful teams and great players. Thinking and talking about the game will make us smarter about our own game and better able to analyze our opponents, but it won't happen unless we make a conscious decision to work at it. Boys especially are hesitant to talk about much of anything, except girls perhaps. Coaches have to demand discussion and guide it well.

Work with a Partner

This pairing allows teammates to know each other better. It also allows work on passing, rebounding, shooting, catching the ball on the move, and communicating. Partners can also challenge each other. The more they push each other, the better the team will be.

Play

Every chance they get, team members need to play together in the off-season, not just settling for summer league games, and not settling for just 5-on-5. They attend open gyms. They find out where games are being played with good competition. They get some teammates together and go. They combine skill development with additional game experience with teammates.

Do Non-Basketball Activities with Teammates

Organize trips to movies, to restaurants, to a volunteer activity that helps those in need or anywhere else that will be fun or productive. If everyone can't go, then a few players should do it with part of the team. Some of the others will go next time. Go to each other's houses and watch movies or hang out. Do whatever the group wants but keep it legal! What takes years to develop can be destroyed with one bad decision. Time spent together will improve all aspects of teamwork and bring the team closer, making the team tougher during the season.

The following additions are courtesy of Tom McCormack and Assistant Coach Bruce Hildabrand's booklet for the Conant High School Cougars basketball team

CONANT COUGAR BOYS' BASKETBALL PROGRAM
OFF-SEASON *GREEN LIGHT* PLAYER DEVELOPMENT PLAN

An Example of a Template for a Program's Essential Philosophy

The FIST

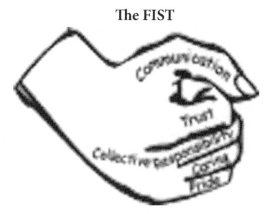

A closed fist is always stronger than an open hand.

Great basketball teams are a FIST, five separate fingers that come together and close themselves into a single unit. The following five assets make up the FIST. We have to work to develop these qualities in ourselves as individuals and as a group during the off-season. They will give us the strength to handle the difficulty of next year's schedule. A closed FIST is always stronger than an open hand.

COMMUNICATION

The thumb holds the fist together. When we talk and tell each other the truth, we will improve the other four areas along with our play on the floor.

TRUST

We must trust each other to do whatever is necessary for the team. Run the floor, take a charge, dive for a loose ball, leave a party. Whatever it is, know that your teammates will do it for you and let them know that you will do it for them.

COLLECTIVE RESPONSIBILITY

We win and lose together. No one individual turns the ball over; we all do. Those are our rebounds, our loose balls, our shots. We don't let any opponent take them from us. Every team here at (school name) is part of a proud tradition. We owe it to those who came before us, and those waiting to join us, to make a positive contribution to that tradition.

CARING

We care more for our teammates than we do for ourselves. This care makes sacrifice easy: taking a charge or making an extra pass to get a great shot instead of a good one. Each individual sacrificing for the team is what we want to achieve.

PRIDE

Doing all of the above repeatedly will develop pride. We cannot be proud of what we do once, but showing the ability to do difficult things over and over again or to do the little things necessary to achieve excellence is something to take pride in. We are part of a tradition of pursuing excellence and taking pride in that pursuit. We want to ensure that all (name of school) basketball players can be proud of what we add to the tradition of (school name and nickname) basketball. (The FIST, et al paraphrased from *Leading With the Heart*, Coach Mike Krzyzewski, Duke University)

SUGGESTED BALLHANDLING WORKOUT

Big Ten Ballhandling Drills (20 Minutes)

2 min	Between the legs	Back to front and front to back from both sides
2 min	Behind the back	Side to side and acceleration
2 min	Spin moves	Both hands—down the middle, to the wing, to the baseline and off the baseline
2 min	Isaiah (rapidly between the legs)	Leg circles and figure 8s
2 min	Machine gun	Behind the back and butterfly
2 min	Backup dribble	Front drop step to crossover into every forward. change of direction move.
2 min	Crossovers and big crossovers	Explosive changes of speed and direction
2 min	Butch Lee moves	Fake crossovers
2 min	Two ball drills— hi/lo	Between the legs, behind the back
2 min	Creative	Challenge yourself and each other

NOTES

Pair your moves up. Make one move complement the other.
For example, add a between the legs dribble
to advance the ball after a pullback dribble.

OFF-SEASON *GREEN LIGHT* PLAYER DEVELOPMENT PLAN
FOR FRESHMEN AND SOPHOMORES

Suggested Shooting Workout—150 Shots and 70 Free Throws

Stretch and warm up	Start in close and move out to the arc slowly. Do not count this part for your shooting total.
Shoot 10 Free Throws	
All Around the Arc	25 jump shots off the pass or spin
Shoot 10 Free Throws	
Off the Slide	25 jump shots off the pass or spin simulating a spot-up shot
Shoot 10 Free Throws	
Off a Screen	25 jump shots off the pass or spin simulating coming off a screen
Shoot 10 Free Throws	
Pull Ups from the Arc	25 shots off the dribble. Rebound and put in any misses
Shoot 10 Free Throws	
Finishes from the Arc	25 shots from Triple Threat, Jab and Pump Fake. Rebound and put in any misses.
Shoot 10 Free Throws	
Post Moves	25 Shots. Spin the ball to the mid-post and practice our entire sequence. • Turn and face, shot; Turn and face, rip through, power dribble, shot • Turn and face, step to the middle with a dribble, jump hook • Quick spin
Shoot 10 Free Throws	

NOTES

Put your totals on your calendar.
Have your partner rebound and pass. Concentrate on moving.
Get your feet and hands set. Step into your shot and following through.
Offensive rebounders: Follow the flight of the ball, while staying in mid-stance and holding position, and anticipate where it will come off the rim.
Concentrate on making a good pass to the shooter.
Pass accurately to the shooting pocket.

OFF-SEASON *GREEN LIGHT* PLAYER DEVELOPMENT PLAN

Shooting Goals Worksheet

First and foremost, the off-season is about developing the skills and strength to become a better player. What do you need to do to reach that goal? Create a specific plan to reach your goals. Need help? The coaching staff is here to help you create and implement your plan.

	GOAL	ACTUAL	SIGNATURES
April Shots/FTs			
Shooting %			
May Shots/FTs			
Shooting %			
June Shots/FTs			
Shooting %			
July Shots/FTs			
Shooting %			

	GOAL	ACTUAL	SIGNATURES
August Shots/FTs			
Shooting %			
Sept. Shots/FTs			
Shooting %			
Oct. Shots/FTs			
Shooting %			
Nov. Shots/FTs			
Shooting %			

_____   _____

Coach's Signature   Player's Signature

REFLECTION

TOM McCORMACK & ASST. BRUCE HILDABRAND

Shooting is the third component of our plan. The plan calls for 100 shots and 50 free throws a day, six days a week. These goals total over 2,500 shots and 1,250 free throws a month which puts the Green Light requirements well within reach. Here are the shooting requirements for completing the program. These are minimums. Feel free to surpass them.

1-Sport Athletes — 10,000 shots and 5,000 free throws
2-Sport Athletes — 7,500 shots and 3,750 free throws
3 Sport Athletes — 5,000 shots and 2,500 free throws

The important thing to apply is the quality, not the quantity, for our workouts. Concentrate on proper fundamentals during the entire workout. Be properly warmed up. While warming up, start shooting within 3-4 feet of the rim and move out to the arc. Do not count warm-up shots toward your total.

These shots can be spot-up 3s, jump shots off the move or off a screen, pull-ups off the dribble, finishes or post moves in any combination. Shots must be charted on a calendar and the calendar signed by a coach once a week. In order to get a signature, there must be a weekly total. Only one signature is required for the month of August. Shots taken during a week without a coach's signature do not count toward the total. If you know you're not going to see a coach to have your chart signed, communicate so an extension occurs.

At the end of each month, add up your weekly numbers to determine your monthly totals and record them on the page with your weight training totals. As the off-season progresses, add the monthly totals together to determine your season total and record.

More about shooting within today's game:

In his 63-point playoff performance vs. the Celtics in 1986, even though there was a 3-point line, Michael Jordan did not attempt one 3-point shot. Not one. Today, some players attempt more 3-point shots than entire teams did back in Jordan's time. Statisticians have researched to determine what players like Jerry West, Oscar Robertson, Pete Maravich, and other great scorers of the past might have averaged with a 3-point line. Would that line have made them different players? The answer to that question is anyone's guess, but we believe those players' effectiveness and overall skills would have been undervalued over time.

What is the difference between a great shooter and a great scorer? Great scorers of the past were usually either back to the basket post players, a rarity today, or excellent ball handlers who were very good at making a pullup, mid-range jump shot, or finishing a drive to the rim. Nowadays, the most consistent scorers are capable long-range shooters with excellent ball handling skills. Those particular skills allow them to create a high percentage shot without the use of a screen, either at the rim or deep on the perimeter. The skills being practiced the most are ball handling with creative finishes, a deep spot-up or a step-back 3-point shot. These are valuable skills, but there is so much more that can be utilized in the game, especially at the high school level.

Within most of the current professional and college metric systems, many coaches actually discourage the 2-point mid-range shot. They want shots in the paint, at the rim, or in certain spots with rhythm 3s. The most common type of screen set for these players is a ball screen. Some programs still use various types of screens off the ball and emphasize post play, but they are becoming fewer and fewer, and everybody has a ball screen play designed for shot clock situations. Wisconsin has had great success running their "Swing" offense where all five players play in the low post and on the perimeter. Most offenses today, however, are a version of either "5-out" or "4 out-1 in" or two designated ball screeners. Use of the 3-point line for spacing is a priority, emphasized more than good screening and movement off the ball.

At a basketball clinic I once attended, former Temple coach John Cheney said, "I would rather have a good shooter take a bad shot than a bad shooter take any shot." At times I honestly asked a player, "Why did you shoot that?" and often the response was, "I was open." My response was, "There is a reason why the other team leaves you open." Did you ever notice how the ball always seems to find the players who can't pass well, shoot, or score? Just because a player is unguarded does not mean that player is open. Players are open to shoot if they have the ball in an area in which they can score. Likewise, just because players are being guarded does not mean they are not open, if they have the skills to create a high percentage shot. Very few shots are going to be wide open, especially for the better scorers on the team. The ability to take and make the "semi-contested" shot is what makes a scorer proficient and dangerous. Great offensive teams often emerge with those types of scorers.

Players practice and develop great offensive skills in the off-season. Once players exhibit those talents, something happens. Other teams will try to make it much harder for scorers to even touch the ball, let alone shoot, dribble, or pass. Here is where footwork and intelligence, using and setting screens, cutting, posting, and heady play define the truly consistent and dangerous offensive threat. For example, if a team likes to switch all screens, then set one to create a mismatch either in the post or on the perimeter. The best all-around scorer understands those situations.

Ballhandling must be a part of every workout. 15-20 minutes daily is the recommended minimum. If it isn't possible to do 15-20 minutes on a particular day, don't skip ballhandling. Do whatever is possible. Ballhandling is a great warm-up activity. Remember, we must challenge ourselves when we handle the ball. Simply repeating the same moves over and over will not help us improve. We need to try new things, chase the ball down when we mess up and keep working. Losing the ball periodically is a sign of progress since it can mean the player is working hard enough. The goals for our players were to make the ball an extension of themselves and to avoid looking at and thinking about the ball. Then, we can concentrate on team execution. Again, ballhandling must be a part of every workout. Basement floors, garages, patios serve as substitutes if a gym is unavailable.

Closely related to ballhandling skill is proficiency at passing and catching. Don't take these for granted or assume that players will be good at them. We will not become good at passing and catching without working on passing and catching. Work on them as part of every workout. A vital part of offense is the ability to deliver the ball on time and on target. Half of every made shot is the pass that sets it up. As passing skills improve, so will shooting percentages. If a workout is done without a partner, Maravich drills, tipping off the backboard or a wall, or imaginative and fundamental ways to develop these important skills can substitute. Fundamentals for passing and catching are in the Preparation chapter.

Weight training is the second key to off-season improvement. We must consistently work at increasing our strength and athleticism. The weight room is not only for varsity players. The sooner we start, the sooner we will achieve positive results. We have an excellent program that includes computerized goal setting and result tracking. On the back of the page prior to each month in the calendar is a page with space for weekly totals. Each Friday write the weight and number of repetitions for your third exhaustion set for the lifts listed on the sheet. There is a formula to convert these numbers into a single rep. max so that total weight can be calculated. See a coach for this formula. At the end of each month, write the total weight of your one rep max for the three lifts and the total improvement since the end of last month in the space provided. In order for a varsity player to earn a Green Light shirt, the three-lift total must reach a pre-determined goal set by the coach and the player. If you need help getting started, talk to a senior or a coach. The more the goals are achieved, the better our defense, rebounding and conditioning will be. Our screening will also improve as will our shooting and overall quickness. Team toughness will increase. In other words, improved strength will enhance every aspect of our game.

A Few Thoughts about Trends

At the high school level, the vast majority of the players will not earn college scholarships. Most young people won't even play in a competitive sphere after high school. Coaches have to try to match what players work on in their summers to what they will expect from them during the season. As Bo Ryan said, "Plan your work and work your plan." Moreover, coaches should avoid choosing a system of play just because it is today's trend. Today's trends on offense are penetrate and space. 5-out, 4-out and 1-in, dribble drive, the blocker-mover system, some ingredients from Paul Westhead's run-and-gun at Loyola Marymount from 1985-1990, and plenty of ball screens with isolation spacing, similar to the Euro-ball screen continuity offense that many pro and college teams use. Recent trends on defense include the "pack line" that has evolved from Dick Bennett, formerly at the University Wisconsin-Green Bay. His son Tony has continued using that system at Virginia. Other trends include John Cheney's tenacious matchup, Duke's coach Kryzewzski's tough pressure/denial man-to-man defense, and Syracuse Jim Boeheim's 2-3 zone. Whatever system of play coaches employ, they should learn everything there is about that system. Self-educate.

If and when the shot clock is a nationwide standard in high school basketball, coaches who have not worked with the shot clock will have to self-educate even more. Studying college and pro basketball movements and offenses might be a good start since the shot clock exists at those levels. There is the possibility that the shot clock will add more scoring once coaches design practices to a more up-tempo pace and players become more proficient in the Big 3. The shot clock also can alter team defenses. For example, there seems to be less full-court pressure with the shot clock. Moreover, coach Dick Bennett was a pressure denial man-to-man coach before the advent of the shot clock. After the shot clock became the rule, he devised his pack-line defense. That type of defense actually slows the game down. On offense, fewer teams will be able to slow the ball down for extended periods of time, especially when outmanned by opponents, but there also might be more ragged or uneven play where teams are uncertain about who should get the ball in critical moments. Just as the introduction of the 3-point shot in 1987 took time to become the norm, so too will the shot clock take some time to become more natural to high school players and coaches. In contrast, European hoopsters have grown up playing basketball with a shot clock. Perhaps that reason and their attention to developing the fundamentals of the Big 3 are why there are more and more European players playing in the NBA.

Simply put, when coaches choose their system and style or pace of play, they have to make sure it matches their players' skill sets and that their defensive style of play matches their offensive style. In other words, it does not make much sense to play a defense that speeds up the game with an offense that slows it down and vice versa. High school coach Bill Schaefer put it this way to us in the early 1970s, when he spoke about trends with a coach's purpose for teaching his system, "Basketball is a smorgasbord; choose what your players can digest, then go kick their ass on game days…by 1 point or more." Enough said.

Off-Season Workout—Varsity

The following workout is courtesy of Tom McCormack,
and is more challenging than the previous one.

BIG 5:
SKILL—STRENGTH—
ATHLETICISM—CONDITIONING—
ATTITUDE

INDIVIDUAL AND PARTNER WORKOUT:
LIFT—TRAIN—
TEAM—PLAY—
STUDY

20 min	Ballhandling	5-minute minimum with 2 basketballs
200	Shots	In 8 segments of 25, all timed with a stopwatch. The goal is to increase the number of made shots and lower the time of the segment.

SHOOTING SEGMENTS

25	Spot up around the arc	Establish workout intensity level
25	Around the arc off spin and slide step	Simulate penetrate and kick
25	Around the arc off spin and sprint	Simulate coming off a screen
25	Spin and catch at the arc, triple threat jab step—pump fake and finish at the rim	Both 1- and 2-foot finishes with pump fakes, mix in finesse and power finishes—rebound any miss before it hits the floor and finish
25	Hard pull up bank shots	Approx. 8-10 ft. from right and left wings
25	Creative and mix of the previous	i.e., Floaters
25	Alternate 1 go to post move and 1 counter move	Both sides
10	Free throws after each segment	The first 2 or 3 will be a game situation with blocking out, fatigue being a factor, the last 7 or 8 will be a recovery period grooving your shot leading up to the next shooting segment. Record your shooting totals and time, and immediately start the next segment.

NOTES

- At the end of the workout, you will have taken 200 shots, 80 free throws, and done 20 minutes of ball handling (all in about one hour).

REMEMBER:
The workout is about quality, not quantity.

- Be sure to use a stopwatch on the shooting segments to simulate game conditions. The workout done with a stopwatch is also a great conditioner.

- At least once a week, test yourself by attempting to make eight or more 3s in a minute, and then immediately three free throws. Being able to do this consistently is an indicator of game proficiency and dominance from the 3-point line, clutch free throw shooting, and a true work ethic.

- Pay attention to staying fundamentally sound, especially in your shooting mechanics.

REMEMBER:
Practice makes permanent not perfect;
perfect practice makes perfect.

- On a calendar make sure to chart your daily totals for ballhandling, shot attempts, makes with stopwatch times, and free throw attempts and makes.

- Six days a week is recommended. Take one day to just recuperate and be with family and friends. If you are a multi-sport athlete, train at least two days or more per week. You can also cut the shooting segments in half and do half one day and half the next, if your time is limited. At the beginning of November, you will have daily, weekly, monthly, and the entire offseason totals recorded. You will be amazed by your totals, your skill level improvement, and your game conditioning readiness.

PERIMETER PLAYERS—INDIVIDUAL WORKOUT

The following two workouts are courtesy of Tom Anstett.

The focus is efficient work for one hour. A player can work longer, if desired, but retain the same focus. It is preferable if Coach Anstett walks you through this schedule a couple of times so you understand the expectations. Study, know, and apply the following guidelines for good training:

- RECOMMENDED: a good jump rope which you do for 5-minutes. Jumping rope is part of the warm-up, but not part of the actual 2-minute segments.) Jump off two feet, use alternate feet, do double jumps, etc.

- There is NO walking during the entire workout; run to the targeted spot for the 2 minutes. Run after your free throw rebound and run back to the line; then slow down and follow your ritual.

- One to three dribbles maximum into any shot. From the low post, use only one dribble.

- Any dribble from the low post is halfway up the knee or the mid-calf. To execute this dribble, you must stay in a mid-stance.

- Keep chin parallel to the floor and keep a wide base upon catching the ball inside and executing the shot attempt.

- This workout can be done with a partner which extends the time.

- Any post-up in the low post is a loud, verbal command, "HERE!!"

- Each game shot is a 2-minute segment with the goal of at least fifteen attempts.

- The hour of time does not include stretching.

- Preferable to do this workout a minimum of four or five times a week.

- IMPORTANT: Keep good habits as you do this workout. If you can't do the full workout, build up slowly. The key is to do each skill at game speed. If you do this training right, you will tire. Once you feel tired, go some beyond that point to build toughness and stamina. Eventually, you will surpass the hour.

WORKOUT

2 min	Ball slaps, two-hand ball pounds into the floor	Vary the height
2 min	FTs for 10 attempts	
2 min	Dribbling: 2 dribbles forward; 2 dribbles back	Switch hands after dropstep
2 min	FTs for 10 attempts	
2 min	Dribbling: change of pace from half-court	Speed dribble back to start; repeat No shots.
2 min	FTs for 10 attempts	
2 min	Dribbling into layups, mix change of pace one time, use pull back dribble next rep, continue to alternate	Finish with layup; shoot different layup each time
2 min	FTs for 10 attempts	
2 min	Intensity Layup	One minute from elbows; one minute from 3-point line
2 min	FTs for 10 attempts	
2 min	Dribbling from half-court, all with off-hand	Speed dribble back to start
2 min	FTs for 10 attempts	

24 Minutes Done

2 min	Spin the ball to the top of key, catch and pivot, ball at shooting pocket—shot fake to quick dribble into lane for a pull up shot.	
2 min	FTs for 10 attempts	
2 min	Spin to the top of the key or wing (can alternate)— catch and pivot, long jab step to shot	No Dribble
2 min	FTs for 10 attempts	
2 min	Spin to the top of the key, all off-hand.	Use a change of pace dribble to a layup.
2 min	FTs for 10 attempts	
2 min	Spin to the top of the key, all off-hand, stutter dribble to a pull up J (in or just out-side of lane)	
2 min	FTs for 10 attempts	
2 min	All off hand from ¾ court— speed dribble to 3-point shot from high elbows	
2 min	FTs for 10 attempts	
44 Minutes Done		

2 min	3-point shots off the catch (or spin)	Pick the spot
2 min	FTs for 10 attempts	
2 min	3-point shot off a long jab	No dribble
2 min	FTs for 10 attempts	

52 Minutes Done	

6 min	*If you work with a partner:* Game of 1-on-1.	Top of key with maximum of three dribbles.
2 min	FTs for 10 attempts	
	OR	
6 min	*If solo:* Pick a favorite move off the drive for 3 minutes, then with a jump shot finish from same area for 3 minutes.	
2 min	FTs for 10 attempts	

NOTES

You have shot 150 free throws...your percentage is?

WANT SOME EXTRA WORK?
50 pushups, 3 minutes of wall-sits, 3 minutes of planks, etc.

> *"Great people are working while the mediocre ones are sleeping."*
>
> ~(the late) Joe Newton
>
> York High School Cross Country Coach
>
>
> *"If it's to be, it's up to me."*
>
> ~George Raveling
>
>
> **Take responsibility for your own improvement.**

POST PLAYER INDIVIDUAL WORKOUT

The following workout is courtesy of Tom Anstett.

The focus is efficient work for one hour. A player can work longer, if desired, but with same focus. It is preferable if Coach Anstett walks you through this schedule a couple of times, so you understand the expectations. Study, know, and apply the following guidelines for good training:

- RECOMMENDED: a good jump rope which you do for 5-minutes. Jumping rope is a part of warm-up, but not part of the actual 2-minute segments. Jump off two feet, use alternate feet, do double jumps, etc.

- There is NO walking during the entire workout; run to the targeted spot for the 2 minutes. Run after your free throw rebound and run back to the line; then slow down and follow your ritual.

- One or two dribbles maximum into any shot. From the low post, use only one dribble or no dribble.

- Any dribble from low post is halfway up the knee or mid-calf. To execute this dribble, you must stay in mid-stance.

- Keep the chin parallel to the floor and keep a wide base upon catching the ball inside and executing the shot attempt.

- Any post-up in the low post is a loud, verbal command, "HERE!!"
- Each game shot is a 2-minute segment for at least 15 attempts.
- The hour of time does not include stretching.
- Preferable to do this workout a minimum of four or five times a week.
- IMPORTANT: Keep good habits as you do this workout. If you can't do the full workout, build up slowly. The key is to do each skill at game speed. If you do this training right, you will tire. Once you feel tired, go some beyond that point to build toughness and stamina. Eventually, you will surpass the hour.

WORKOUT

2 min	Hand slams on ball.	Bring the ball to the hand and increase the temp as time progresses. Then, slam the ball on the floor with two hands.
2 min	FTs for 10 attempts	
2 min	Mikan, forward for 60 seconds, then reverse for 60	
2 min	FTs for 10 attempts	
2 min	NO BALL—catching on balance (heel to toe)— arms up, half-step to catch— stay in stance—inside pivot to face basket	Always yell, "HERE!" Go from block to block.
2 min	FTs for 10 attempts	

2 min	With ball—spin to the catch, pivot to face basket, keep ball in chin area, shot fake of 6 inches—drive to hoop with 1 dribble for layup and score	Alternate blocks
2 min	FTs for 10 attempts	
2 min	With ball—spin to catch, drop step to baseline, stay in stance, 1 dribble to power layup off 2 feet	Alternate blocks
2 min	FTs for 10 attempts	
2 min	Spin to a catch, jump hook	Alternate blocks
2 min	FTs for 10 attempts	
2 min	Spin to a catch to mid-post, pivot to face, shot fake, drive to hoop with 1 dribble	
2 min	FTs for 10 attempts	
2 min	Low post spin and catch, pivot to face, no dribble—jump shot	Use glass
2 min	FTs for 10 attempts	
2 min	From the high post, catch and pivot, jump shot	Follow so you end with a score, if shot is missed
2 min	FTs for 10 attempts	
2 min	From the high post, catch and pivot, shot fake, drive to layup	

3 min	**If you work with a partner:** Game of 1-on-1 from low post, make-take
2 min	FTs for 10 attempts
3 min	Game of 1-on-1 from high post, make-take
2 min	FTs for 10 attempts
	OR
3 min	**If solo:** Catch at wing(s), pivot, shot fake, drive to score, 1 or 2 dribbles.
2 min	FTs for 10 attempts
3 min	Same from the top of the key
2 min	FTs for 10 attempts

Last 10 Minutes

2 min	Dribbling—no shots—change of pace, up and down the floor
2 min	FTs for 10 attempts
4 min	Work on favorite low-post move
2 min	FTs for 10 attempts

NOTES

You have shot 150-160 free throws...your percentage is?

WANT SOME EXTRA WORK?
50 pushups, 3 minutes of wall-sits, 3 minutes of planks...

Take responsibility for your own improvement.

CLOSING THOUGHTS ABOUT SHOOTING

*"You can coach guys to play defense, to run your plays.
You can't make them into shooters during a season."*

~Red Auerbach
(qtd. in *Let Me Tell You a Story 280*)

Shooting is the one skill that most players would choose to occupy their time. To become proficient at it, however, a casual occupation of time falls far short of the attention and understanding of the details that need practice.

Techniques for teaching and practicing the components involved in building and mastering shooting are detailed in the Preparation and Attentiveness sections. Some additional ideas about shooting follow, specifically as they apply to games and competitive game like drills. Shooting practice and drills need to be tailored to enable the best shooters to get looks at the rim from their release point, efficiently, quickly, and often. Remember, most defenses will be designed to limit the number of touches these players get either completely or in their favorite (also scouted) scoring areas on the court. The drills need to be as close to "game speed" as possible. Hopefully, the players who are more often the drill winners are also the receivers of last-second shot opportunities in games.

Players will have both good and bad misses. Are the misses short or long as opposed to right or left? Short or long misses are better and more easily corrected than right or left. The faults of consistent short or long misses are usually in the legs; right-left misses are harder to diagnose because several factors come into play. Elbow action and follow through are involved. Do missed shots consistently grab a lot of the rim, or go halfway in, before coming out and landing close to the rim? There is not much to be corrected here that a few hundred correct repetitions can't fix. Or do most misses hit hard on the rim and land somewhere outside the lane? This type of miss takes diagnosis by the coach or specialist who can teach the subtleties and corrections in shot mechanics. The follow through on the shot is like a person's signature, something to take great pride in. A consistent and solid follow through is the primary indicator to a good or bad miss, which is crucial to a shooter's mentality. Good makes or misses keep the shooter believing that the next one is going to go in. Every other mechanic may be in place, but without belief, inconsistency and doubt are practically guaranteed. Faith and hope are both great virtues to possess. A shooter with a consistent follow-through has faith. A shooter with an inconsistent follow through only has hope. Daily shots in the hundreds, not just a few, are the requirement for the prospective scorer. Also, what do makes look like? Consistent swish, back rim, or other? Elbow lift, arc, rhythm, trunk rotation, release point, follow-through, and ball rotation are points to study. Where are the eyes on the release and follow through?

All players need to understand the freedom and limits of their shooting range, and the types of shots they are able to make at an acceptable percentage. The coaches determine those factors. Shooting percentage is the key component. Other than 5-on-5 scrimmage situations, percentage is primarily determined and developed in game-like shooting drills and games. We have had several great players-shooters who rarely lost playing H-O-R-S-E, but in games were not able to either get a shot attempt or make the ones they could. These reasons are why shooting drills and games need to put pressure on the shooter as a live game.

We have heard the old saying, "If it's not broken, don't fix it." This adage applies to those unorthodox shooters who can really score. Again, the focus here should be on shooting percentage and the ability to get and make not only the open shot, but also create and make the semi-contested shot. Shooting range and area of the court are main points to identify with this player. If a program starts teaching shooting mechanics before high school at camps and clinics, coaches will have less confusion as to the dilemma of choosing between fixing the technique and risk hurting the player's confidence or leaving them alone.

There are times that shooting mechanics need to be practiced without the competitive component to refine and reinforce certain actions involved in the shot. Players at the first or second level of the aforementioned workouts need to realize that this is a mental review and rehearsal, not a shooting workout.

Shooting from too far away can alter proper mechanics. Range will increase with proper mechanics, proper weight training, and physical maturity. Even more mature players will make the mistake of shooting too far away from the rim, especially early in a workout. This is one of the main reasons we emphasize doing twenty minutes of ballhandling prior to a shooting workout. This assures the shooter warms up properly.

Players should not fall into the trap of trying to constantly adjust or change their shooting mechanics. Many young players have a tendency to experiment with their shooting mechanics. Each adjustment is a step back at first. Some players pick up this habit watching games on television or on the Internet. Coaches need to monitor and critique players' shot mechanics regularly in and out of season. The best players for them to imitate should be the older players in the program who have established the correct mechanics and habits.

A one-dimensional player or move can be scouted and taken away. Both post and perimeter players must develop a primary move and a counter for that move. For the jump shooter the ability to go both right and left into a shot is both basic basketball and a move to build more creativity for getting the shot against any defense. Players adept at creating off the dribble need to master shot fakes, pass fakes, eye fakes, and foot fakes as setups to the drives into pullups, floaters, or finishes at the rim. For the post player, the ability to jump hook middle, then pump fake up and under are two primary weapons. Drills from triple threat position can emphasize certain moves. With the right work and time, most players can develop a couple of these for game effectiveness. The ones who are good at all or most of them are pretty special.

 REFLECTION

TOM ANSTETT

Currently an outstanding assistant coach at Marquette University, Rob Judson was a terrific shooter at Zion-Benton High School in Illinois and during his playing career at the University of Illinois. I had the pleasure to both play basketball with him and coach against him when he was the head coach at Glenbrook South High School in Glenview, Illinois, and I was the head coach at Glenbrook North High School in Northbrook, Illinois, in the 1980s. We were discussing shooting one day and he mentioned that he had a particular habit of thought when he transitioned from defense to offense in games. As he was running down court, he saw the middle ring holding the net as his target for his next shot, a swish. He told me that he did that every time he turned to go on offense. Folks, that is called focus! Great shooters and scorers possess unusual, but fundamental habits within their training and mental preparation.

 REFLECTION

TOM McCORMACK

Players who completed our off-season program were awarded a "Green Light" shirt, a symbol of their accomplishment in the off-season. The check-in periods allowed us coaches to monitor various things, one of them being shooting mechanics in relation to the types, intensity level, degree of difficulty, areas, volume, and shooting percentages of the shots as they related to the season. The "Green Light" shirt was a very valuable tool that helped us mold the type of shooters and their individual shot selections we wanted in our program.

Free Throw Shooting

There are some theories about this skill, but it is never just another drill. The way foul shooting is today, it seems like some coaches treat it as "just another drill" when foul shooting will always remain a true staple of the game and an accurate reason why games decided by eight points or fewer are won or lost. Free throw shooting at practice must be as game like as possible. From season to season, percentages may vary. We believe we have been most consistent shooting free throws in games during the season by practicing shooting them immediately following a fatiguing drill.

We shot in groups of three or two players. The first few shots are game-like: the action stops, and the shooter is on the line. We teach concentration on a specific free throw ritual, not the end result. After the first two or three shots, the shooter worked on grooving the shot without any pressure. We did not shoot many, just a few under fatigue (3 shots, 2 shots, or a bonus 1-and-1) and then about 3 to 5 more with less pressure. We only kept count of the initial shots under pressure.

During foul shooting time, the non-shooters practiced our spin blast technique for offensive rebounding a missed free throw. One player stepped into the lane, back-to-back to avoid an over the back call with the defender and try to tip out a miss toward the top of the key. The other player spun under and sealed the other bottom defender, one high and one low. We used a hand signal between our two offensive rebounders, so the action was coordinated. This technique fulfills a preparation point of coaches' having a last-second play after a missed free throw when the team is down by two or three points.

Rich Kolimas at Lincoln-Way East High School in Frankfort, Illinois, employs a 2:30 free throw drill. Each player has a ball with no more than three to a basket. Each player has 2:30 to make ten free throws. After each make, the player retrieves the ball and sprints to half-court then back to the line for the next attempt. If the shot is missed, the player sprints full court, then back to the line. At the end of the time, any player who has not made ten free throws does ten pushups. At other times, Coach Kolimas made every player shoot one free throw each while the rest of the team watched. He felt this activity put more pressure on the shooter. There was a team goal for makes; if the team fell short of the goal after each player had shot, there was a penalty.

Shooting Drills and Shooting Games

Some of the following competitions may be used as both a drill and a game. Fundamental habits are established in the drills, whereas in shooting games, the established habits are reinforced in contests. Some contests are lighter in nature and some are more competitive. In team or group competitions and drills, we either assigned specific matchups or picked captains to choose teams. At the risk of sounding harsh, we never worried about hurting the players' feelings who were chosen last when the players chose the teams. Our team culture had established that this was not a popularity contest. There was too much at stake. Captains chose players solely on the basis of who was the best at getting the job done. If players felt embarrassed about where they were picked, then they could decide to work extra to improve their shooting.

Shooting Drills

In all drills we strive for maximum participation, high level competition, meaningful skill practice and execution, little down time, and communication.

POINTS OF EMPHASIS

On all shots outside the arc, we emphasized that holding the follow through is of prime importance until the ball hits the rim. On all shots taken inside the arc, off penetration, or in the low post, we emphasized following the shot for an offensive rebound.

3-PLAYER SHOOTING

This series of shooting drills can be done as an individual or a team competition with a stopwatch in 2-minute segments. Coaches set three players to a basket, one or two basketballs, one passer, one shooter, one rebounder, each alternating roles on every shot.

The types of shots practiced in this drill are spot-up 3s, pull up jump shots, floaters, bank shots, finishes at the rim off one and two feet, slide 3s off penetrate and kick, shots coming off screens, and post moves.

EXAMPLE-SPOT UP

The shooter spots outside the arc; the passer starts under the rim; the rebounder starts out of bounds. On the pass, the passer closes out the shooter and then replaces him in another spot around the arc, the rebounder becomes the next passer, and the shooter replaces the rebounder. The rebounder may contest shots off penetration. On shots off penetrate and kick, the shooter uses a relocation slide. On shots coming off a screen, a misdirection step to a sprint is practiced. Shots coming off a screen start with a player on each wing and one at the top of the arc who is the passer. Post moves start with a passer on the wing or top, a post player, and a passive or live defender. The passer replaces the defender; the post player replaces the passer; the defender replaces the post player.

At the end of two minutes, the winner shoots a free throw to validate the win. All the losing players do pushups or sit ups while the winner counts. If the free throw is missed, the winner must also do the loser's activity. If this is a group competition to determine a winner, someone from the winning group shoots a free throw and then it's the same as an individual contest. Every time a group member shoots a free throw, a different member of the winning group must shoot the free throw next until all have taken a turn.

30-SECOND SHOOTING

Coaches put three players with two balls. Each player must shoot from three areas: the right and left wings and the top of the key. There is one shooter, one passer, and one rebounder in every 30-second segment. After every shot, the shooter holds the follow through until the ball hits the rim and then slides along the arc a few feet in that area. The shooter relocates after every shot as if their defender helped on penetration. We suggest this drill as a team competition which keeps the rebounder focused on high hands, hustle time, and quick outlets to the passer. It keeps the passer focused on making an on-time and on-target pass. It keeps the shooter focused on proper footwork, hand target catch, rhythm step and release, and follow through. Team competition keeps all the teams competing against the clock. Each make counts as one point. Each team of three keeps track of its totals from each spot. After each team player has taken a turn at a spot, the winning team will count out pushups or sit ups for the losing teams. Then teams moved to the next spot. We also let the winners choose the basket for the next spot. One option is using a counter step to sprint off a screen for the top of the key shots. A suggestion for picking teams is to select captains of similar shooting ability, all either good, average, or poor. Give the poorest shooter of the captain's group the first pick and the best shooter the last pick. Players will quickly discover that fundamental execution and communication on the part of all three teammates will lead to efficiency, consistency, and proficiency.

FIRE IN THE HOLE POST-UP DRILL

We had all players do this drill for 3 minutes. It can be done with three or four players. There is one player outside the arc on each wing at the free throw line extended and a player in the lane. One of the arc players has the ball and starts by passing it to the opposite wing. The passer cuts into the lane and works to post the live defender on the ball side in the lane. Upon establishing position and calling "Here," the ball is passed into the post. The offensive player is permitted one power dribble at most. More than one dribble is a turnover. Whichever player wins the low post battle, that player sprints to the open spot on the arc and becomes the next passer into the post. The ball is passed out to the last post passer who restarts the action with a reversal pass and then cuts into the lane to become the new post player. Once the drill has started, a player must get a defensive stop to play offense. The ball can be passed out of the low post to the post passer on the wing to allow the offensive low post player to repost. If there is a fourth player, the successful player in the post goes to the arc, and the unsuccessful player goes out of bounds with the player out of bounds becoming the lane defender. The ball is never passed into the post without the post player calling, "Here!"

Some Shooting Games for Players:

BEAT (LEBRON)

This game's name depends upon the age of the shooter. Beat Shaq, Beat Candace, Beat Kobe, Beat Michael, etc., have all been popular, but the game is the same and creates pressure on the shooter. This game can be done individually or with a partner. The shooter starts with a free throw worth one point. Any miss is -2 (or -3, -4) against the shooter, but the makes are always one point for the shooter. The game can be played to any point total and the shooter decides the spot and the move. Is it a shot off the pass or is it a one dribble left into the shot? Whatever the decision, the move is the same in any one game and helps players focus on one particular move to practice. One of this game's best features is that in order to win the game and "Beat LeBron," the shooter must shoot over 50% (which should be any shooter's goal when he/she decides to work on shooting). A good game to end a shooting workout because players are more fatigued.

ACCUMULATION

This game is done with a minimum of two players, and we suggest no more than four players, so they get a good amount of shots. Each player starts with 21 points; the first player to zero loses. One player shoots at a time. No layups in this game. Minimum distance is fifteen feet, but each player has his/her own choice of shot. If the shooter makes the shot, he/she yells, "One." If the next player makes a shot, he/she yells, "Two." If the third player makes his/her shot, he/she yells, "Three," but if it is a miss, that player subtracts two from 21 and now has 19. After any miss, the total starts again at zero and "accumulates" from that point. This game gets competitive within the shooter's psyche, especially when players get a streak of six, or eight, or ten, etc. One miss after those totals can wipe out that shooter. Players enjoy this game and it requires a good level of concentration.

(MASCOT) WINS!

This game is a good one for the end of a practice. The winning team supplies the name of the school's mascot once all the shots are made by that particular team. Two teams compete. Coaches select two players to choose their teams. One team at each main basket. Coaches can decide on any total to make at each spot; the spots are a baseline, a wing, an elbow, top of the key-three, and one half-court shot. For example, each team must make five shots total from each of the four designated spots and one half-court shot. Starting with the baseline shot, teams are in one line with one basketball. Each shooter follows his/her own shot and passes to the next teammate in line. Once the team makes the designated total-the shots do not have to be consecutive makes-that team moves to the wing, then to the elbow, to the 3-point shot, then to half-court. After the half-court shot scores, that team yells, "Cougars, Knights, Griffins (etc.) WIN!" Losing team has pushups. Players love it, and it does not take as long to make a half-court shot as you might think!

CALL YOUR SPOT (FREE THROW SHOOTING)

There are five spots to hit on the rim: front, back, right, left, and a dead center swish. To advance, a player has to first call a spot, and then hit that spot on the rim. On all the spots, except the swish, the ball does not have to go in. Concentration and focus must be narrower than a regular free throw in a game. If the ball does not hit the called spot, the player's turn is over. However, he/she does not start over, just waits for the next try. On a hit call, the player keeps shooting. The first to hit all five spots is the winner. This drill forces concentration on the rim and follow through. Players become very aware of the fine tuning and importance of both.

WORLD SERIES (PARTNER SHOOTING)

Two players with one ball, the passer and shooter alternate after every shot. There are seven shooting spots in this drill, structured similar to baseball's World Series. The shooting spots are the corners, low wings, high wings, and top of the key. A player has to make two shots in a row from the same spot to win that spot. A player needs to win four spots to win the World Series. Any time a player wins a spot, the loser gets to pick the next spot. No spot can be used again. Each player shoots one shot at a time. The passer must start under the rim and close out hard to distract the shooter but may not block the shot. It counts as a make if the passer touches the ball or fouls on the closeout. If the pass is poor, the shooter can make the passer repeat the pass. Any shooter picking the low wing spot has the option to call, "Bank," which means all shots from that spot have to be banks by both players to count. Rather than assign partners, we let players challenge other players. Losing players ran the number of lines for the number of games they lost by (4 for a shutout, 3 for one win, 2 for two wins, 1 for three wins). If a series is tied after six games and needs a game 7, there is a vocal group watching that deciding contest. When the last game is done, the losers run all together.

AROUND THE WORLD

The spots are the same as World Series. This game can be played with two or more players, but a small group is best. Each shooter starts in the same corner and gets one shot. On a make, the shooter moves to the next spot and shoots again. For this and all other shots, the shooter has a choice after a miss. He/she can take another shot and move to the next shot on a make. After a miss, however, that shooter must start all over in the corner. Then the next player shoots. If that player chooses not to take a second shot, he/she starts at that spot on the next turn, but the next player shoots. The first player to make it all the way back and make a shot at the first spot is the winner. Coaches can add that a player must swish a free throw to win after going all the way around.

POWER BALL

This is a shooting game in the post. We suggest one minute per player with three players at a basket. The game starts with two balls, one ball on each low post block. The shooter goes from one block to the next, picks up a ball, calls "Here," pops the ball, ball fakes to the middle, power dribble drop steps to the baseline, pump fakes, and shoots a power shot off the glass. After shooting from both sides, the shooter follows the same, seven-step fundamental routine, but then head fakes baseline and jump hooks from the front of the rim. The shooter must keep shooting the same ball on a miss until it goes in before moving to the next ball. The other two players retrieve the made shots and place them on the block. Any first shot made without executing all of these fundamentals first does not count in the shooter's total of points, but pump fakes still count.

Only a make on the first shot counts for two points. The other players keep track of total points and pump fakes; only one pump fake per side counts in the total. After the three players have shot and have a total number of points, each player gets one free throw for each pump fake worth one point each. Players will alternate shooting free throws until each has shot the number earned with pump fakes. The point here is that shots in the post lead to fouls and "old-school" 3-point plays, especially after pump fakes. Note: Good low post players who are good foul shooters are worth their weight in gold. This routine needs to be practiced in drills until it becomes habitual before incorporating it into this shooting game. Any shots or fundamentals of post play that coaches emphasize can be substituted in this game. If the players are matched up equal in ability, the games are pretty close with the winner often being determined at the free throw line.)

Playing 1-on-1

 REFLECTION

TOM ANSTETT

A high school coach once told me when I started coaching, "Being a good one-on-one player and making free throws constitute the altar of basketball. If kids can't do those two things, they don't belong on a team."

That statement was years ago, but that feeling still rings true. So, what are some primary factors in playing one-on-one that develop a player's game? No matter what the game rules are, offensive players should rarely take more than three dribbles on any possession. In that way, players maximize the triple threat position with shot faking and footwork; these three keys are paramount to quality 1-on-1. Playing 1-on-1 gives players the opportunity to incorporate the jab step and/or shot fake to set up the dribble move or vice versa. The fakes provide the offensive player the quick feedback necessary to read the defense and acquire the "quick patience" to make a logical, but fundamental offensive move. A balanced jab step can be six inches or longer with the shooting foot; shot fakes should be short and quick (shooting pocket to the nose-chin area). Multiple fakes might be necessary, but any fake should be aggressive, not rushed. The offensive player should start the triple threat with the ball at the shooting pocket, ready to score. The offensive player tries to attack the defender's front foot with either an onside or a crossover start. The chess game between the two players is for the offensive player to get the defender on his/her heels with the hands down to facilitate an uncontested jump shot or to get the defender too close and too high with straight legs, so that a drive is open for the taking. A strong and smart triple threat, solid faking, and quick starts upon reading the defense will make a slow-footed player much better. Moreover, 1-on-1 can assist players' growth as rebounders.

1-on-1 Options

- Score points like a game: 3 for a 3 and 2 for a 2. Keep the games short. Time them, for example, a maximum of five minutes or five scores, etc.

- Make-take. An alternate form of this game is for the offensive player to keep the ball after a score and is still behind.

- Defensive stops. If the defender stops, he/she gets a point and stays on defense. If a player scores, he/she goes to defense. Scores do not count in overall point total.

- Ball Denial. Have one passer so that the defensive player has to deny the ball and the offensive player has to move to get free for a pass. Use of the back door is encouraged. This form of 1-on-1 helps coaches identify the better defensive players who can adjust quickly to be in the right position so that the offensive player does not cut over the top, leaving the defender behind the play.

- 1-on-1 cutthroat. This drill has three or more players at a basket. In offensive 1-on-1, the offensive player may start anywhere outside the arc in a catch ready position. The defensive player starts directly under the rim, passes to the offensive player, and sprints to a stutter step closeout with a high hand and in a defensive stance. If the pass is off target or too slow, the offensive player can make the defender pass it again. The offense has a maximum of three dribbles and earns three points for a 3-point make and two for a 2-point make. On a made basket it is make-take, but with a new defender. After a stop, the defender becomes the new offensive player outside the arc; the next player out of bounds becomes the next passer and defender, no matter if there is a score or a stop.

- Dribble only with the off-hand.

- Play from the low post only with a limit of one dribble.

Playing 3-on-3

3-on-3 represents one of the best uses of time for improvement as long as the players are playing with intensity and focus. In 3-on-3, contrary to 5-on-5, each player gets lots of chances to handle the ball, shoot, rebound, pass, move without the ball, and defend. A steady diet of 3-on-3, combined with competitive 1-on-1 and plenty of shooting and ball handling, can add up to a fantastic off-season for dedicated players. Throw in a couple of camps and consistent weight training and the transformation in players from June to October can be astounding. We recommend a few ideas for good 3-on-3:

- Each player may take a maximum of three dribbles on the perimeter and only one with back to the basket in the low post.

- Each player should try to make a hard cut or set one good screen before a shot. Avoid excessive use of ball screens.

- Vary the type of game. Use similar games suggested in 1-on-1 above.

- Vary the offensive structure to begin the possessions. In one possession, the offense might start on the perimeter; in another, the offense might start with a ball side triangle.

- Players execute solid 1-on-1 moves within 3-on-3 to improve court vision and passing decisions. On the drive, players create a shot for passes to open teammates. Teammates without the ball learn to space themselves correctly in open passing lanes for the driver.

- Self-motivate for improvement of weaknesses. For example, in one game a player might focus on offensive rebounding, in another left-handed moves, etc.

SUMMER CAMP PHILOSOPHY

As previously mentioned, summertime revolves around individual development. This belief also filters to summer camp organization. In one sense, camps are an opportunity for coaches to attract interested future players from feeder schools in all grades. One approach is for the head coach to organize one-week sessions for camps in grades 2-3, grades 4-5, grades 6-7-8, and high school. These sessions can be run throughout one month in each week. Having varsity and lower level players work with the grade school campers is a great asset. Emphasis on fundamentals, 1-on-1, footwork, 3-on-3, dribbling, shooting, passing, and enthusiasm are necessary instructional pieces. Campers love contests such as hot shot, free throws, spot shooting, and 1-on-1. We recommend 4-on-4 for any full court competition within summer camps. We did not give trophies for contest winners. We gave camp shirts which provided great advertising and were more practical. If budgets allowed, we periodically purchased rubber basketballs with our school logo. Kids loved earning those basketballs. The last day of camp was all competition and contests with some review of the fundamentals for the week. Kids enjoyed those days, and they added a nice touch to the camp experience. In any event, the contests run at the end of the camp should emphasize what your program deems essential and demonstrates what you have taught. Each contest has a time limit of 1-3 minutes, except for free throws.

Here are some samples for the contests which can be run in many ways:

- Offensive 1-on-1

- Defensive 1-on-1

- Offensive and defensive rebounding—Use the 3-person rebounding drill from the rebounding section as a contest.

- Post up—Use the 3-person post-up shooting drill from the shooting section.

- Ballhandling

- 3-point shooting

- Hot shot—This contest is a combination of 3-point shooting, 2-point pull-up jump shooting, and finishes at the hoop. Shots are taken sequentially worth 3, 2, and 1 point.

- Free throw

You also might consider running one-week camps from Monday to Thursday, with no camp on Fridays. A three-day break can be healthy for all involved. Fridays and Saturdays can be open gym days, weight training days, or team tournaments and shootouts.

In addition, the off-season camps are an opportunity for assembling all the players in the program to drill together. By doing this activity, the younger players, especially freshmen, will experience and understand the expectations and the culture in the program. They can get a true sense of what it takes for them to be good players.

June is a critical month. In addition to fostering relationships with future players through grade school camps, coaches lay a foundation for the upcoming season for their varsities. Time structure becomes essential among all the tournaments, leagues, camps, and multi-sport players. Rules vary in terms of contacts with players state-by-state. Sharing athletes is an appropriate discussion between the head football, head baseball, and the head basketball coaches, so that they create mutual trust for sharing time with multi-sport athletes. (We have more detail about sharing athletes in Mentality.)

SUMMER LEAGUES AND TOURNAMENTS

These events are good for coaches to observe progress of individual players and the system for next year, but smart coaches keep in mind that few remember who wins a summer league. A winning summer promotes confidence, but is less important in the big picture, at least compared to individual progress. In the summer leagues, we wanted the players to learn more responsibility. Thus, we liked the captains to coach, so we might observe leadership develop. We did not want parents to be the coaches. They are not at workouts nor do they understand the nuances for the offenses and defenses. We talked after the games. Some head or assistant coaches do not attend their team's games, but if it is an important part of summer progress, those coaches should attend regularly. Moreover, inexperienced assistants should make efforts to attend as well. Sitting next to the head coach in the stands or on the bench and listening to that coach's thoughts are terrific learning tools for any level of assistant. Those novice coaches should keep a journal in order to record two or three concepts they learned from watching the games or from listening to the head coach. Head coaches might also keep journals during seasons, especially using them after games to list both the good and the bad of that game.

Consider replacing one of your summer weekend shootouts with a 3-on-3 tournament or competition within your own program. Invite alumni to attend and even enter a 3-on-3 team of their own.

> *"Champions are made while the stands are empty."*
>
> ~Dabo Swinney
> Clemson University

A Special Note to Players: The Four Levels of Preparation

Coaches, feel free to share these points with your program.

LEVEL 1:
FOOKIN' AROUND

This level sits just above the vegetable. Players in this level play or shoot with no vision or goals. They shoot around; in contrast to the minds of winners where there is no such thing. These players are quick to lose whatever focus they started with and substitute daydreaming, which is not to be confused with imagination. They will return to some shooting but do not really care whether the ball goes in or not. They cannot sustain effort or imagination yet believe they are working hard. This level of player stays comfortable in this level time after time and does not truly care about winning or losing or the ability to compete against the game. If these players make the team in the fall, coaches have to repeat the same things over and over to them and prepare for a rather mediocre season. The most important thing for these players is that their ear buds are working properly. *Grade: D- to F*

LEVEL 2:
PLAYING AROUND

Players in this level possess many of the attributes in Level 1 but sustain their delusion for longer periods of time. These players usually start with no warm-up or purpose, and the slightest distraction turns into a social activity. They think of a goal, but after starting to sweat, lose it. They need water or a break every ten minutes. They rely on shooting shots they have no business taking, nor do they work on ball handling or game situation dribbles too often or too much. They cannot do fifty pushups without crying for Mommy. Hard work is an elusive phantom. They dream of being better but do more talking than actually practicing. Thus, these players develop the "Would a, Could a, Should a" illness: If the coach would a played me more…I could a worked out harder… We should a won, so I blame…" *Grade: C- to D (probably D)*

LEVEL 3:
WORKING OUT

These players possess some good qualities but are not quite at a championship level. They have a goal and can sustain it for quite a while, but has the goal been accomplished? These players might not know every time they work out. They have some imagination and will work here and there on skills other than shooting, but without a firm and consistent application of technique. They take a lot of shots but need more game speed doing so. If this level player works for an hour fairly hard, it is quite an achievement. They approach the point of discomfort, but rarely surpass it. These players are willing but need more direction with more 1-on-1 coaching. There is much less (but still some) "would a" and "could a" with these players. Many high school players fulfill, but rarely surpass this level. *Grade: B to C*

LEVEL 4:
TRAINING

Great imagination, goal setting and evaluation, and concise application of details in techniques are qualities for this level of player. Out of the seven-day week, these players work out hard at least six of the days and make no excuses. They are responsible for their own improvement; they might not even need a coach or trainer. They will work efficiently for a shorter time than spend more time and get less done. The workout is well-planned. Warm-up, intensity levels, specific skill/strength/agility work, and cool down are all parts of the planning process. When fatigue strikes, they are not finished; they accomplish a bit more. These players believe they are never outworked. "I will, I can," and "I do" eliminate the "would a and could a." Not very many high school players consistently live in this rarified air, except for the thoroughbreds. Grade: B+ to A

Players who wish to be considered as "go-to's" need to be Level 4 workout fanatics and consider the skills necessary to be that key player at the end of game, quarter, and shot clock situations. An old saying seems particularly appropriate: What came first, the chicken or the egg? Players in this pressure role have to possess an assassin's mentality. Is the ability to shoot more important than the ability to create a scoring opportunity off the dribble in this responsibility? One is not complete or nearly as effective without the other. In these situations, defenses will in all likelihood be designed to stop these players, or at the very least make it difficult for those players to make a play. "Assassins" have to be able to first get the ball, get to a certain spot and/or in triple threat position, and attack and shoot at the appropriate time. In most cases the shot will be at least semi-contested. In the hands of average players who live In Levels 2 and 3, this shot is at best a prayer, better than no shot at all, but kind of like playing the lottery. In the hands of the "go-to" player this is a high percentage, practiced, well executed strategy. The split-second decision that the "go-to" player must make also has the factors of time and score to apply. The most important decision is whether a semi-contested shot is the best option or whether a pass to an open teammate is better. Ultimately, last-second situations boil down to reading the defense well and trusting teammates. Level 4 players prepare for those moments physically and mentally, mainly in the off-season.

In what level is each of your players?

# G – GUTS

"Do opposing teams dread being guarded by your team?"

~The Authors

*"Stop by stop by stop. Play aggressively. Sprint back on 'D'
and pay attention to how we're supposed to guard as a team."*

~Gregg Popovich
San Antonio Spurs

POINTS TO PONDER

In World War II General George S. Patton's nickname was "Old Blood and Guts." Even though the backdrop for this book is not war and Patton was determined to stay on the attack, playing great defense night in and night out requires a similar mental and physical approach. Hence, we focus in this section on defense, the unsung and many times ignored part of playing basketball.

What does sound defense require from the coach? In three words: instruction, commitment, and relentlessness. From the player? Toughness and intelligence. Not every player is tough or wants to play defense, nor is every coach committed to producing a great defensive team. Consequently, in today's game from the NBA on down, some teams run up and down with minimal structure, cast up contested shots or three's, drive for uncontested layups, loaf back in transition defense, fail to block out for rebounding, and commit a multitude of other sins. In those systems, the lack of discipline which demands players play like a team at both ends is missing in action. Teaching and insisting on great team defense accomplish three main values:

1. Players understand the meaning of commitment and sacrifice.

2. Players earn loyalty to each other when they fulfill distinct responsibilities.

3. Players become a true team.

A good defensive team is a sign of inspirational team morale and faith in the program. Good defense covers for a multitude of limitations on offense. Good defense takes intelligence and effort. No matter what particular defense a coach decides to employ, the application of that defense is a non-negotiable. There are no nights off from playing outstanding "D." None. In a quality program, that feeling runs in everyone's veins, right down to the managers. A loyal fan base will follow, too.

SOME "A-B-Cs..." FOR STRONG DEFENSE

A = ANTICIPATION AND AIRTIME

Bob Knight said, "It is better to anticipate than to react." Anticipation is the key to a good defensive mind and a good defensive team, so coaches must train their players' minds to anticipate where the next pass will be going, what the opponent with the ball will try to do. Scouting will assist anticipation but cannot replace a player's readiness and alertness to anticipate. Airtime means the correct movement of the defenders when the ball is being passed, i.e., in the air. Are the defenders ready and in the right spots on the catch of the pass by an offensive player? Five must move like one during airtime; this movement is a yearly tenet for coaches to drill into players, no matter the defense or the talent level.

B = BUTTS DOWN

Being in stance and staying in it need correct practice with a heavy dose of determination and guts. The head of the defender stationed just below the shoulders of the offensive player with the ball is a solid school of thought for the stance. Players have to learn to bend the knees, not the waist. Bending at the waist hinders good balance and vision. Guarding the ball is tough enough even with good balance.

C = COVER TWO

Is each defender in the right spot in order to cover his/her opponent or area in a zone and guard the basketball? While showing help in gaps, every player has the responsibility to know where the ball is and to be able to provide early help and recover. Recovering is what the good/great defensive teams do well.

D = DEFENSIVE TRIANGLE

Similar to the ball side triangle of offense is the defensive triangle of Ball, Defender, and the Defender's Assignment. Throughout his coverage of college basketball games, Dick Vitale refers to this principle as Ball-You-Man. The defenders off the ball always need to be in position to react early, no matter the defense. This mindset of anticipation and reaction requires defenders seeing both the ball and the positions of their responsibilities. We referred to this action as Point the Guns. One hand points toward the ball; the other hand points to the player or area that particular player is guarding, with the body's position in the middle of the triangle at an angle deep enough to enable them to see both outside points of the triangle with little to no head turning. Pointing the Guns in the right position is a foundation of any defensive drill in practice, along with the communication standard of Early, Loud, and Often. Another reason for the Ball-Defender-Defender's Assignment triangle is to put doubt into the ballhandler's mind as to whether a trap is coming. A good bluff and backup move can be as effective as an actual trap, especially against a shaky ball handler or passer. We want the ball handler to feel like a long-tailed cat in a room full of rocking chairs. Most dribblers will feel very comfortable one-on-one, with the floor cleared out and every defender right next to the player they are guarding.

TYPES OF DEFENSES

Man-to-Man Defense

A man-to-man team makes decisions. Which two of Coach Bennett's three defensive points are you going to emphasize? What are you going to allow? What are you going to take away? Coach Bob Huggins, head coach at the University of West Virginia, teaches his players to force the ball into a box and make the box smaller to force offenses to operate from the baseline corners. Denial teams like to force the ball to the baseline because they typically front the post and thus are in a position to help or trap the baseline drive. Teams not concerned about denial don't want the ball going to the baseline because they usually defend the post from behind and are not in a position to help. They are not concerned about ball reversal as long as it is high and wide on the perimeter. Probably the biggest decision is how aggressive you want to be in terms of denying passes, stopping dribble penetration, or allowing ball reversal. Other points for decisions are: ball pressure, pick up points, amount and timing of switches, coverage for screens on and off the ball, forcing baseline or middle, guarding dribble handoffs and brush screens, defensive stance in ball/gap/help positions, guarding the post, dribble penetration, closeout hand placement and reaction, and box out and loose ball reaction. Individual assignments and adjustments like trapping, help rotations, or recognition and defending of isolation and special plays etc. need to be practiced and communicated through scouting. Who is your defensive stopper? If you have one of those special players, consider yourself fortunate. It's tough to neutralize the other team's best scorer without those valuable players who can deny the ball, take away dribble penetration, contest the shot, and box out their assignments with fierce determination and pride. This type of player is akin to the boxer Rocky who always seemed to find his reserve against Apollo Creed's superior skills and power. Playing against a team with several types of these tenacious defenders is a physical and mental challenge. A pressure denial team can take a screening team out of its offensive pattern and force dribble penetration and back cuts as the offense's only options. A pack line defense may allow a team to run its offense and reverse the ball, and with application of a good scouting report, may bend but never break its commitment to no transition scores, the denial of rhythm 3s, penetration, post up baskets, and second shots.

Zone Defense

There are several types of zones but basically two options, no matter the disguise: an odd-front look and an even-front set. The matchup zone in reality is a switching man-to-man defense. Similar to the man defense, zones can be the base defense of a dominant program's philosophy or used as a changeup curve ball, trying to disrupt the balance of a stronger team. Some teams are great at attacking the man defense but become unglued or passive attacking a cohesive zone. Zones can be aggressive, scrambling, trapping, or controlling gaps and protecting the rim. Some try to be a combination of schemes. The ball-gap-help principles still apply, as does early-loud-often communication. Scouting the other team's strengths is crucial, because in a zone, individual matchups are constantly changing. The zone defenders must know the skill sets and tendencies of everyone on offense. They must know the strong and weak points in the zone they are playing and be able to cover for each of them. Defensive rebounding can be a problem, especially for the odd-front zones, but there is a two-edged sword with this issue: the rebounding can be erratic, but once the defensive rebound is secured, zone teams are in a prime position to fast break and/or attack any pressure because the players are approximately in the same spots to run in their lanes. Practice of the various slides, angles, coverage areas, and rebounding responsibilities of all zones is essential. In either a man or zone defense, contesting shots is a constant emphasis. High school coach Bill Schaefer said, "Sometimes there's nothing like a nice little zone to do the trick."

Presses

Why do teams press and trap? Philosophically speaking, two types of presses exist. One is to increase the pace of the game, and the other is to slow down the pace of the game. Steals, deflections, poor shot selection and disruption of the offense are the main goals for most presses. For some teams, their press is their offense. What are the ways to set up a press? The best way is to score. Other ways are in free throw huddle situations, substitution after the last made free throw, time outs, dead balls, and quarter breaks. Some teams are good at pressing in defensive transition off a miss or turnover, but this transition takes practice and great communication.

Trapping

Please do not teach this aspect of defense UNLESS there is pressure on the ball! Ball pressure is a must. More credentials for a good trap are coordination between trappers, communication, and anticipation. Trapping players want to squeeze the player being trapped while the dribble is being used or is still a live threat. The trappers must avoid being split or driven around. Getting behind the ball, with not one but two players, puts the defense at a numerical disadvantage. Once the ball is dead, a good trap becomes a vice.

Who?

Two spirited, yet disciplined players with some length and smarts, if possible. Never use three players in a trap. Two interceptors and a rim protector are the three players not in the trap. We recommend the distances of 1/3 off the guarded player and 2/3 distance from the ball. These guidelines are especially essential when rotating behind the trap. Interceptors must learn to attempt a steal on immediate air-time of the errant pass and open up with the outside arm to swipe a pass. Using the wrong hand-and missing the pass-gives an advantage to the offense. Rotation remains a crucial factor for a good trapping team since not every trap is successful. Question: How quickly do players need to rotate into, out of, or behind a trap? Answer: When they go to bed and turn off the light on the wall, they should be in bed and under the covers before the room is dark. Let the players think about that one.

What?

Approach an offensive player in some prime spots on the court and lock-in, even interlock the legs so that they form a two-sided box uncomfortable for the ball handler. Either the dribble or the pass can be victims of a good trap.

Where?

Ideally, there are eight spots for traps. In the back court, the corners and the immediate corners before the half-court line are ideal. Four more spots are the two corners across half-court and the two corners at the far offensive end. Those four frontcourt spots can put the offensive player into a complete box with the sideline and baseline acting as defenders. Trapping in the middle of the court is a bit difficult since the passer has too many options to release a pass. However, a trap in the middle can be an element of surprise.

When?

Traps can be sprung at any time in a game, but many times are best after free throw makes or in presses. Traps can be employed in a run-and-jump defense by turning the dribbler toward the alley with another defender coming from behind to trap as the offensive player dribbles toward the sideline corner over half-court. Players can trap off ball screens, too, or trap the post player upon the dribble inside.

Why?

Change the momentum in a game. Help a team overcome a deficit. Speed up the tempo to the defensive team's liking. Force the offensive players who are trapped into mistakes with bad passes (preferably soft, lob passes out of the trap) and deflections. Take away a certain player or an area of the court. Surprise an opponent.

How?

Two players approach with a sprint-to-slide technique. They should not have to run cross court to trap. The player guarding the ball contains the dribbler until his/her teammate arrives to form the trap. The two defenders try to inter-lock their legs and not allow any splitting of the trap. Above all, they cannot foul in a trap, unless time and score dictate. They should create a wall with the arms up, but not break the invisible plane so as to reach in and foul. Once the trap is established, trappers must mirror the ball to deflect or force a soft pass. Trappers must take away escape space: on any pivot by the offensive player, trappers should close in the vacated space and not allow the player trapped to regain that space. The trappers want the offensive player to make the errors. If the offensive player who is trapped raises the ball above his/her head, the two trappers should slide closer to the ball handler, even force that player to turn his/her back to the action so to lose even more vision. If a pass is thrown out of the trap up the court, the two trappers must turn and sprint to the ball line to be in help or gap position. The trappers can never stand up straight, turn up their heads to watch "the fireworks," thinking their jobs are done. The next pass after the pass out of the trap is their target. Don't use a denial stance vs. a player you want to trap; bait the offensive player into making a bad pass. In the half-court, passes to the wing and baseline are ideal ones to trap.

OFFENSIVE AND DEFENSIVE TRAPPING DRILL

There is one ballhandler against two trappers. The area is the half-court, side-line to sideline with the baseline and half-court line out of bounds. A coach anywhere in the half-court starts by passing the ball to a player on the side-line. The ballhandler's goal is to beat the two trappers and cross the other sideline with a balanced, two-foot jump stop. Any time the ball handler is trapped, he/she may pass to the coach, but then must cut to get the ball back and still get to the other sideline. The goal of the defense is to get the dribbler under control by working together and not getting the corner turned or the trap split. Ultimately, trappers try to force the handler to pick up the dribble which makes the trap even more effective. If the dribbler passes to the coach and the pass is deflected, the defense wins. If not, defenders deny the pass back from the coach. If the pass is completed, the drill continues.

This is also a great ballhandling drill that we made all players do. It will reveal who worked on their handles in the off-season and expose those who didn't. Instruct the trappers to show no mercy.

A DRILL FOR INTERCEPTORS

One defensive player is at the top of the key, and two offensive players straddle the arc at the opposite free-throw lines extended. A coach starts at half-court with a ball and dribbles directly at the defender. The defender chops his/her feet, reads the eyes of the coach, and slide/sprints to intercept or deflect the coach's pass to a wing.

The coach does not fake, just looks first, then passes. We are trying to build positioning and anticipation reaction in the defender. Any intercep-tion should be with two hands. Any deflection should be with a downward swiping action with the outside hand, as in denial, so the defender can recover to a defensive position on the receiver if the pass is missed or recover the deflected ball, rather than just knock it out of bounds.

Some More "Gutty" Thoughts from Coaches to Players:

- Don't ask teammates to do what you don't.

- Taking the charge is an undervalued skill and promotes a team's willingness to dominate and intimidate the opponent. It can change the course of a game and symbolizes a team's togetherness, toughness, and unselfishness. The mindset and technique are similar to setting good screens.

- Gutty defenders master blocking out and are the first to the floor for loose balls.

- Gutty defenders are team leaders in taking charges and blocking shots. Scottie Pippen is a fine example for that type of defensive leadership.

- A defender trying to deny the ball to a good scorer must learn to stay in the footsteps of the offensive player around screens. That denial requires energy and toughness.

- The first priority for guarding a shooter with the ball is to take away that shooter's release point by keeping a hand above the ball.

- Always a "What's next?" mental approach, play after play.

- Do not ask why in a game. That question is useful after a game.

- The majority of fouls are mental errors. Most fouls are committed 3-4 seconds before the actual whistle. In a majority of cases, the fouling player is out of good stance, unalert, out of position, or just plain lazy. Showing those fouls on video is a helpful teaching tool to assist a team's improvement to avoid needless fouls and to keep an opponent out of the bonus for as long as possible.

- Being in great shape is a must for point guards and post players. Oh yes, everyone else too.

- A possible defensive decree for a team: "No Shot. Bad Shot. One Shot."

- Incorporate drills that take players out of their comfort zones. When the players get proficient in those drills, add more discomfort.

- A coach can tell how tough players are by looking at their knees and elbows for floor burns. Scrapes speak truth.

- Hands on knees usually means closed mouths. Players are thinking how tired they are. Can your team communicate on defense when it is fatigued?

SPECIAL SECTION #1:

Guarding the basketball is the toughest job on defense but can be the most inspirational to a team. If a defender can stay in front of the ball for three or four seconds, there is a good chance he/she will stop penetration, frustrate the flow of the offense, deflect a pass, and/or contest the shot. If a defender happens to be guarding James Harden of the Houston Rockets, that poor soul should be prepared to stay in front of the ball for 15-22 seconds or until a second helping of popcorn is desired. In either case, a hearty, tough disposition for that particular defensive player is required.

Defending a great shooter requires the defender to know, or at least quickly figure out, three factors about the person they are guarding. First, the best way is to deny the ball to the great scorer. Second, consistent high percentage shooters have a very specific release point, which if altered, drastically affects the shot attempt. Third, for many scorers the path the ball takes to the release point is just as crucial. Once the player has the ball, cushion, hand placement, and knowledge of the aforementioned factors are the defender's primary weapons to take away a shooter's release point and shooting rhythm. If denial of the ball does not occur, the defender's primary goal should not be to block the shot, but to contest it as well as possible. "Thou shalt not foul the jump shooter" is one of the Ten

Commandments of basketball. Several factors come into play, but knowledge is the power which can lead to a poor shot by the shooter or no shot attempt at all.

A suggested model for defenders on the ball is as follows:

- Stay in front of the ballhandler without help and keep the head below the offensive player's shoulders.

- Upon the catch by an offensive player, that defender should yell, "Mine!" or "Ball!" to establish ball coverage. We like the word "Mine," because it reflects a strong mental approach. In either case, the defender must yell something to convince his/her teammates that the ball is covered. A good defensive possession always begins with tough defense of the ball and early-loud-often communication.

- Force a ballhandler in an east-to-west movement, denying any north-to-south penetration.

- Force the ballhandler to pick up the dribble, then yell, "Dead! Dead! Dead!" A garlic and onion breath is advisable. A bad mood helps too.

- Stay body-to-body with a strong mid-stance, keeping the eyes on the opponent's mid-section or on the basketball, dependent on the coach's system. The distance players need to effectively guard the ball is called their "cushion." Tough defenders can stay body-to-body with little or no cushion. Coaches need to determine how close their players can guard the ball without hand checking or fouling, take away the release point and/or contest a shot, or deny dribble penetration without gap help. It was not a compliment to be known as a "big cushion" defender.

- Mirror the ball with the hands and a wide base.

- Get a 5-second call, deflect a pass, or force a bad pass. It is very nerve racking for a ballhandler who is constantly dealing with a defender in a very tight cushion, who constantly forces the referee to chop a 5-second count.

- Guarding the ball handler, always a top priority, is taken to another level against teams that feature the dribble as their primary weapon and where, by design, the entire offensive structure contains dribble options. On some teams one or two players dominate possession of the ball with the dribble. Attacking with dribble penetration into the lane, ball screens, and/or dribble handoffs on the perimeter almost completely takes the place of screening off the ball, passing, and posting up.

- As Hamlet once said, "To reach or not to reach. That is the question." Then again, there really is no question for this aspect of defense, only one answer: NO reaching or fouling!

This job requires very special players. Having those players allows any defense to flourish. We used a drill called "3-Lane Zig-Zag" to develop the required mindset and skill. The coach divides the court into thirds the long way from baseline to baseline. Ballhandlers must stay in their lanes and get to the other baseline. On the sides of the court, the defender keeps trying to force the ball to the sideline. In the middle the defender plays straight-up and tries to force the ball out of the middle. Each player goes on defense and offense three times. Early in the season or in the drill, players should keep hands behind their backs on at least one trip to emphasize proper footwork, stance, and voice. Any time a player gets beat off the dribble, they sprint and recover. The goal at the end for the defender is to keep the dribbler from crossing the baseline in their lane. As an added plus, this drill requires good ball handling and game-situation dribble moves.

SPECIAL SECTION #2:

With good length, quick jumping, and most importantly, a sense of timing, some players can become proficient shot blockers. An element of patience is needed along with the "pane of glass theory." Blocking a shot requires the defender to wait just long enough for the shooter to leave his/her feet and commit to the shot without leaving the ground prematurely on a pump fake by the offensive player. Then, that defender tries to jump straight up to tap the shot to gain possession and even better, start a fastbreak. Even though the crowd might go berserk, the defender should avoid slapping the ball hard into the third row and some fan's cheesy nachos. Consequently, it takes a good shot blocker to get possession of the ball after the block, a Bill Russell specialty. Avoiding fouling when attempting to block a shot takes practice. Players can imagine a pane of glass between their blocking hand and the ball. In this way, the shot blocker will not take errant swipes at the ball, bringing the arm too close to the shooter's hand or body. Patient self-discipline is the key to not fouling for the shot blocker. Even though some fouls will occur with an active shot blocker, with experience those precious defenders will save some victories.

Blocking shots in the air isn't the only way to change a game. When defending or helping close to the basket, players can learn the low block, especially the guards. This technique has been very effective for us over the years and can be taught and practiced in three ways: sprinting to catch a player driving to the basket in transition, defending a taller player in the post who likes to dribble or bring the ball below the waist, or digging in and helping in the post. In transition the defender uses the inside hand to swipe with a downward motion while continuing the sprint to avoid body contact. In the other two, a jab and recover step is used with the same hand action. This defensive maneuver should only be used as a secondary step of defense. Don't let players use the technique as a crutch instead of moving their feet and getting in primary guarding position. (That type of player is known as a hack.) Emphasize the difference between reaching/fouling and solid low block execution. A favorite offensive maneuver employed today by many drivers to counter the low block is covering the basketball like a football running back. Michael Jordan was even known to slap his own arm in hopes a trailing official would hear the slap and call a foul. The chess game never ends.

SOME FAVORITE DRILLS TO DETERMINE THE "GUT-PASSION" OF PLAYERS

PECKER DRILL

One fantastic drill and the least known. Fantastic for the coach, at least. This drill features competitiveness, quickness, cleverness, and stamina. We also need to mention "killer instinct!" Two players face each other in the key area about 15' apart. They have the half-court boundary for the contest. One player chases the other. Time is 30 seconds. The player being chased has to run and elude the "pecks" on the shoulder by the chaser. Key point-the player being chased will lose big if he/she runs at the same pace and in the same direction. He/she has to use changes of pace and quick cuts to avoid being constantly pecked. The running and cutting are constants. Encourage no stopping. The chaser counts aloud the number of pecks in thirty seconds. After the time elapses, the players switch roles with no more than five seconds between the chasing. The loser stays on, and the winner advances to compete against another winner. Just think, a coach can run a "Pecker Drill Tournament!" Very good for early season conditioning. Coaches will discover who has the guts to stay on task. Coaches might discover certain players who can hound an opponent/scorer into the ground when it is necessary. Money-back guarantee: Coaches will be able to evaluate each player's level of conditioning and ability to persevere.

THE CORRECT DEFENSIVE SLIDE

We are not sure how coaches miss this fundamental, but we see it again and again. In their defensive stances when guarding the ball, what foot do your players move on the first dribble? This correct slide requires focus, guts, and stance. Players must lift and slide the outside foot, the foot in the direction of the first dribble. If players dribble to their left, their defenders are lifting their right foot/leg as wide as good balance allows, and vice versa. To enable a quick change of direction, players use short, choppy steps and avoid bringing their heels together. Keeping that correct slide a constant avoids needless fouls and ensures that the defender is covering ground to stay in front of the ball and deny penetration. This fundamental must be taught, drilled, shown on video, and demanded by coaches. Idea: have the players do the correct slides in the same manner as a four-line drill.

PASSING FOR POINTS

Use 4-on-4 in the half-court. Coaches select captains and the captains choose their teams. This drill is high intensity both physically and mentally for the players and the coaches. One coach has the offense and the other coach has the defense. The objective for the offense is to complete perfect passes to the triple threat position or score. The objective for the defense is to disrupt or deflect any pass attempt while not allowing any scores or offensive rebounds.

The offensive goals are to improve basic screening and receiving screen skills, proper types of passing and pass receiving, floor spacing, shot selection, and offensive rebounding. The defensive goals are to improve denial, get deflections, and disrupt offensive play. Loose ball anticipation and recovery, "gang" defensive rebounding, and early-loud-often communication are constant emphases.

The drill is played in three segments with the winner being the first team to get 21 points. The offense scores by completing passes in the following ways: one point for a catch coming off a screen, two points for a catch after setting a screen, two points for a made 2-point shot, three points for a made 3-point shot. If the offense turns the ball over, it goes back to zero and gives up possession, goes on defense, or is replaced on defense by a waiting team. A team must reach a total of seven points first, and then it must score a field goal to "lock-in." No points are given for the lock-in field goal, only a lock-in status at seven. If a team is able to lock-in, it keeps possession and now tries to lock in at 14 by the same rules and then at 21 (same rules) and score to win.

There are no ball screens allowed, but they could be incorporated if it is a part of the offense or a teaching point. "Locking in" means that if a team fails to score and "lock in" at 7 or 14 points on its possession, it drops down and starts again from where it locked in previously. If the defense deflects the ball in any way (pass, drive, shot) but does not gain possession, the offense keeps the ball and drops back to zero or its previously locked in spot at 7 or 14. It is also a great offensive rebounding drill because so much is riding on the ability to keep possession if a shot is missed.

Coaches' tasks: The offensive coach awards passing points based on the cleanness of the pass, triple threat on the catch, spacing rules, or the emphasis in the offense. The coach will count out points and call out when a lock-in situation is reached. Players will quickly realize that the best way to lock-in is to build up points via the pass, rather than to attempt to score without breaking the defense down with ball reversal first. Our code for reversing the ball was, "Touch three sides," meaning a minimum of three reversals. The defensive coach actively hounds the defense to deny, deflect, be disruptive, block out, and finish the possession with a stop and the ball. The coach decides whether to call fouls. We usually called hard fouls because the drill often gets physical. Lock-in possessions are particularly intense. Coaches can have the players shoot free throws on shooting fouls in a lock-in situation.

The drill will instill:

- **ON OFFENSE:** ball reversal, go-to scorers, quality possession time, shot selection (both from where and by whom), and the tough mindset it takes to finish possessions in tight, intense game situations
- **ON DEFENSE:** the determination, skill, and communication necessary to play great intense defense for a sustained period and the resiliency to hang in and bounce back as well as lock-down defenders

At times in practices or in real games, all we said was, "Pass for points," to focus players into the right mindset for offensive and/or defensive execution. Great offensive possessions, offensive rebounding, and free throw shooting are primary ways to stop any momentum the other team establishes. Great defensive possessions that end with a stop are momentum shifts. The teams that combine both in each half of games are usually in for a great season. This drill was a tremendous team builder for us. Early in the season, teams would struggle to earn even a seven-point lock-in. As the season progressed, the efficiency increased in this drill where teams developed the skills and teamwork to increase the point totals to 14 and eventual 21-point lock-ins. This drill revealed stages of improvement that transferred to games. Keep in mind that we used a maximum of twelve minutes for this drill.

4-ON-4 AREA PASSING

The 3-point line is the boundary with 4-on-4 teams. There is no shooting. The team on offense has to complete ten passes without a turnover. If they succeed, they must stop the other team from doing the same for a victory. Cutting, crisp and correct passing, screening, catching, triple threat are all prime skills. No dribbling. An offensive player must throw a pass to a different teammate from the one who threw the pass. There are versions too: one dribble each, no screening, just cutting, the area is the lane only, etc. Excellent for communication, intensity, ball handling, defense, and toughness.

THREE STRAIGHT STOPS

In 4-on-4 half-court "Shell," the defense must get three or more straight stops before they can be on offense. There are key points in every close game where a team has to respond on defense and get three or four straight stops to stem an offensive run or get control of a game when the coach cannot call a timeout. Three straight stops are a good defensive goal for each quarter in four-quarter games. For games played in two halves, coaches can determine the standard for a consecutive stops goal in each half.

VEGAS

Half-court form of a delay game. 5-on-5 with the offense having to complete ten passes without a turnover. There is no screening; players rely on cutting to get open. Emphasis on high and wide spacing. Because the defense needs the ball, there is no responsibility to protect the rim. Important: an offensive player may not pass to the teammate from whom he/she received the pass. The only shot allowed is an uncontested and made layup which counts as one point. The offense keeps the ball. Coaches will find it an interesting concept as to what players determine as "uncontested." A coach can say that any scored layup costs the defense the game, too.

ALLEY DRILL

The court is divided into two halves vertically. Players pair up: one as the ball handler and the partner as the defender on the ball. Coaches should be sure that the defenders get their outside foot on or over the sideline to keep turning the dribbler. One exception is the defensive philosophy of forcing the ball to the sideline, but then the same idea holds for the baseline.

3-ON-3 (4-ON-4) STOPS

The only way a team wins is the number of defensive stops. If the offense scores, its reward is to go on defense.

3-ON-3 FULL COURT

Do you desire to see what your players can do and what they are made of? 3-on-3 full court is one terrific answer. Great for early season, open gym, Christmas break, or anytime. Conditioning, offensive skills, full court passing, half-court execution, shot selection; you name it, and that skill is involved. Limit the number of dribbles by each player on offense once the ball is over half-court. Time the game or make it a score and stop or a stop and score contest. There are all kinds of versions that will test the mettle of your players.

3-ON-3 PARALLEL PASSING

3-on-3 starts on the baseline and goes to the other end. No shooting. Suggest putting the point guards in the middle, but that does not have to be a constant. The offensive players have to free themselves to pass the ball up the court beyond the 3-point line or into the low post. Once that is accomplished, the offense gets a point and the defense has ten pushups. New 3-on-3 starts. Do not allow cross court passing; the ball has to be passed to the middle to be reversed. Each defender is denying the ball. Each pair of players must stay in their lanes. The player in the middle has the width of the lane in the full court. The wings have lane to sideline(s). Variation-once the ball crosses half-court, players play live 3-on-3. Coaches find out a lot about their players in this drill: who can deny the ball? Who can cover in transition? Who talks? Who hustles? Who can pass well under pressure? An important teaching point in any full court transition situation is "ball line." That concept requires defensive players who are not guarding the ball to sprint ahead of the ball's location, so they are ready to gap and/or help. "Ball line" refers to the imaginary line across the court even with the ball. Defenders need to be ahead of the ball, not behind it, no matter where the ball is. So often, if players are not guarding the ball, they have a tendency to daydream. In this drill, there is none of that.

THE "NO TALKING" DRILL (COURTESY OF PAT SULLIVAN)

On occasion, make 4-on-4 teams and do not allow any talking on defense while they play cutthroat. Tempers will rise when players are caught in tough situations that could and should be avoided by better early-loud-often communication.

For example, a player gets blasted from behind by a good backscreen or gets blindsided by a ball screen. This drill just might convince players about the importance of talking on defense.

REFLECTION

TOM ANSTETT

Before the United Center in Chicago, there existed the Chicago Stadium. To that arena I often ventured to watch college doubleheaders or earlier Bulls' teams. When Dick Motta was coaching the Bulls, they strung together some excellent years. Their rocks were guards Norm Van Lier and Jerry Sloan. You never witnessed tougher defensive players or better leaders. They never gave an inch to opponents. I recall one particular night when I sat in the upper rafters of the Stadium. Sloan had five fouls and was guarding a tall post player on the block. Sloan did not want to foul out, so he guarded the center with his arms behind his back, sliding his feet like a mad tiger up and over the opponent when the ball was at the wing. If the wing tried to throw it to the post, Sloan darted around the player, either catching the pass or knocking it away. I was enthralled. Sloan played with such desire and that night was one such example. His mantra was his defense, every game. By the way, he didn't foul out. (Note: Jerry Sloan passed away on May 22, 2020. His influence will remain.)

REFLECTION

TOM McCORMACK

We talked about guts often as a mantra for our defense. Without the guts, our three main calls for defensive positions did not matter too much, but here they are. We used the same three calls no matter if we were in a man or a zone defense.

- "Ball" for the player guarding the ball. Two tasks: affect any shot attempt and deny dribble penetration

- "Gap" for the two players nearest the ball. Tasks: help on penetration and be early in Marine time: If you're not early, you're late!

- "Help" for the two helpers who see it all. They are the charge takers.

Whatever a head coach chooses for the team's main defense as the talent dictates, commit to it, teach the hell out of it, and do not waver from it.

Defense contains a few basic techniques, a ton of commitment, plus will and intelligence from the players.

BONUS DRILL-MONKEY IN THE MIDDLE

Two offensive players stand about ten feet apart. One defender is between them with a ball. The drill starts with a pass to either player who may not dribble. The defender sprints to a stutter step with a high hand closeout to the player with the ball. The goal of the defender is to affect the quality of the pass without fouling. The offensive player executes good triple threat and passing techniques. The defender gets out of the middle by deflecting passes or forcing a certain number of bad or soft passes. Add a degree of difficulty by allowing the offensive players one dribble. This drill will reveal a player's disposition to dominate or falter as fatigue and frustration levels mount.

"Those to whom defense is not important
will have the best seat in the game."

~Rick Majerus

 # R – REBOUNDING

*"If you're not going to rebound,
then take your butt off the floor and out the door."*

~LeBron James
Los Angeles Lakers

*"I always laugh when people ask me about rebounding techniques.
It's called just go get the damn ball."*

~Charles Barkley

*"Most of my rebounds came from positioning,
where I was able to get the ball while in heavy traffic."*

~Bill Russell
Boston Celtics

TOM IZZO'S FIRST PRACTICE

Do you know what Michigan State head coach Tom Izzo had his team do at their first practice of the 1999-2000 season? No shooting drills. No ballhandling drills. No defense, no rebounding, no passing, and no sprints. At the first practice he had his players practice cutting down the nets. That's right. They practiced cutting down the nets! It must have worked because less than six months later Coach Izzo and the Spartans did cut down the nets at the RCA Dome after they beat Florida for the national championship. Success can be a self-fulfilling prophecy (www.usab.com/youth/news/2010/08/inspirational-stories-from-the-nba-players-top-100-camp.aspx).

Original and creative but cutting down nets after a championship game victory does not happen without relentless and timely rebounding. In terms of this fundamental, some teams like the Boston Celtic-led Bill Russell teams in the 1960s built their entire mojo on their defensive rebounding. Others go the opposite way where most of the offense relies on the quick shot followed by pounding the offensive glass. Whatever your philosophy lies, or if it is halfway between those two patterns of play, this chapter will embolden your team's improvement at rebounding.

POINTS TO PONDER

- "Ultimately, rebounding is about taking charge." Bill Russell

- If everyone blocks out well, a shot will come off the rim and hit the floor before the defense secures the ball.

- Rebounding becomes one of the very few aspects in basketball where selfishness is good. Players who consider themselves rebounders will not get every rebound, but they should darn well try.

- Why are some high school, college, and NBA coaches not concerned with blocking out? A lack of respect for the game and lack of instruction of its fundamentals are a couple of reasons. A third is "entertainment over execution." Missed shots in basketball occur 50% of the time, so why not make defensive rebounding and blocking out a priority?

- Rebounding becomes a nasty business. Players get pissed off at one another and at their coach. Coaches cannot shy away from players' tempers in those moments but use them to motivate players to board even harder.

- Combined with a reliable point guard, rebounding retains its position as a top asset for controlling a game, even in contests where teams might shoot poorly.

- A strong defensive rebound is the start of the offense.

- The better shape players are in, the better rebounders they can be. Better shape transfers to multiple efforts to gain possession of the rebound. One cannot dismiss or take lightly the physical nature of play on the glass.

- Technique is less essential than attitude. Wanting the ball is the first part to a rebound…and the grand finale.

- If blocking out is not drilled every day, at the very least it must be hounded and emphasized by coaches and team captains.

- Do you want a tall, weak player who shies away from the glass or the short, hostile one who will do anything to win, including block out and outboard the bigs?

- The majority of rebounds are secured below the rim.

- Good balance is a prime ingredient to acquiring and holding good position and successful ball security. You cannot find many great rebounders who get many boards with their legs together. Balance and a mid-center of gravity help to hold a position, whether offensive or defensive. This concept carries more weight when a player rebounds in a crowd.

- A player's consistent ability to rebound in a crowd exhibits toughness and desire. That player is a treasure.

- There is no one true statistic that measures a player's desire to rebound, no matter the time of game or the conditions, home or away.

- Great rebounding starts with a good shell defense and ends with a contested shot and the ball in the hands of a mobile, agile, and hostile defender.

- How many games are lost due to second and third shots by the offense because the defense is careless when the ball leaves a shooter's hands? In close games or after last-second shots, the rebound, not the first attempt, often determines the fate of both teams.

- The lack of free throw defensive rebounding is one of the primary causes of games lost by fewer than eight points.

- Long shot = long rebound.

- Rebounder is a terrific role for the right player.

- The initial outlet pass is fundamental to a strong finish at the other end. Overhead or baseball passes are recommended. Chest passes are too slow, unless the receiver is less than fifteen feet away. If a defensive rebounder can secure the rebound while turning in the air to face the sideline and the potential receiver before hitting the floor, that team has a better chance to start a fastbreak. At times, defensive rebounders can find themselves trapped or attacked after they secure the ball. In this situation, the rebounder should use one power-out dribble to split the double team and create an opening for the outlet pass. The power-out dribble is a long dribble on an angle out and up the court. It finishes with a two-foot jump stop in order for the rebounder to throw an accurate outlet pass.

- Coaches can use football blocking pads in rebounding drills to toughen their rebounders. Who holds onto the ball? Coaches should also devise scrimmages where all rebounds count as points.

- If a team gets twenty defensive rebounds in a game, then that team should have 8-10 offensive boards in the same game.

- In the '90s during the Chicago Bulls' championship runs, Dennis Rodman had seven games with twenty rebounds and NO points. Moreover, many times he was guarding the opponent's top scorer or best player, no matter the position. Think he was valuable?

- Very few teams can call themselves championship caliber without tough rebounding at both ends, despite the flurry of 3-point shots today.

- Fierce rebounders intimidate opponents. However, if a player's fight for position results in a muscle contest, that player often will lose position and vision of the ball.

- Defenders guarding shooters and yelling out, "Shot!" on the attempt alerts teammates to "Find-Stick-Sustain" the block out. In the event that the defenders lose inside position, they should try to push the offensive players out of bounds or under the rim by getting back-to-back so to avoid any on-the-back calls. Any defender who makes it a habit of losing position requires more enjoyable, blocking out drills or needs more bench time.

- Emphasize short, choppy steps going to the rim after the perimeter block out. Too many players elongate the steps, lose the block out contact, and give up the long board. This is an important teaching point due to the increase in 3-point shooting.

- Paul Silas could not jump well, but he ended his NBA career as one of the all-time leading rebounders. Timing, intelligence, and positioning were his rebounding traits at both ends of the court. The "Paul Silas" move for offensive rebounds from the block literally takes the defender under the basket because when the offensive player goes under, the defender tends to release block out position. At that point the offensive player slides under the defender for inside position.

- A note for all rebounders: Know the percentages! Corner shots- 95% of the time rebound to the opposite corner or back to shooter/90% of the shots taken from the top rebound back to the top. Those two percentages tell the defensive block out player where he/she wants to drive the offensive player. Wing shots-unpredictable, but 65% of these shots rebound to the weak side, thus emphasizing the importance of weak side rebounding.

- Forearm and hand strength should be an emphasis in weight training for rebounders.

 ## REFLECTION

TOM ANSTETT

In high school I had one game with 36 points and 27 rebounds of which ten were offensive. I was prouder of the rebounds than the points that helped us win that game. As I progressed in junior and senior years, if the opponent scored any layup, I took it as a personal insult against my family. I wanted to block the shot, take the charge, or intimidate. Then get that ball. That progression was quite the advancement from my sophomore year when my shot was usually blocked, I shied away from taking a charge, and I was intimidated far too often.

TEAM DRILLS

For any rebounding situation, there are two scenarios. One is blocking out the shooter and the other is blocking out everyone else. When blocking out the shooter, a defender's first priority is to take away the shooter's rhythm release point, then contest the shot. On the shooter's first step after the shot, the defender executes the normal block out technique. For the non-shooters, defenders use the forearm-pivot technique.

HAMBURGER
(EARLY-SEASON)

Three players, one ball, no fouling on shots, but fouling allowed on rebounds and on attempts to strip the ball. The coach throws the ball off the board and the players compete. The first man to score three baskets is done. Instant offense on any rebound. Two dribbles are allowed. Have a trainer handy.

BALL IN THE MIDDLE
(EARLY SEASON OR ANYTIME TO REVIEW
IF THE TEAM BECOMES SLOPPY ON BLOCKING OUT)

Five players in a circle on offense and five inside of them on defense. The ball lies on the floor in the middle of a circle. The coach or one offensive player yells, "Shot," and the offensive players work to secure the basketball; the defenders hold block outs for 3-4 seconds before securing. The goal of the defenders is to locate and sustain the block out.

SLIDE REBOUNDING
(ALL SEASON)

This rebounding drill is run 4-on-4. The offensive players space themselves outside the 3-point line and the defense starts in the key. The defense will slide from side to side, and then a specific defender will close out on a shooter. The rest of the players must communicate and find a player to box out before securing the rebound.

Purpose:

This drill gives players experience communicating, boxing out, and pursuing the basketball on a rebound. It also works on 3-point shooting.

Setup:

- 4 defenders inside the key.

- 4 offensive players outside the 3-point line.

- The coach starts with a basketball at the top of the 3-point arc.

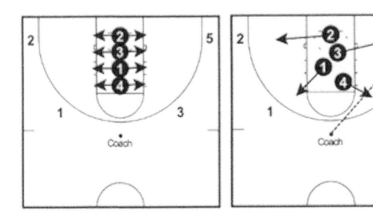

The drill begins with the 4 defenders sliding side-to-side in the key.

After a few seconds, the coach passes the basketball to one of the offensive players and calls out the name of one of the defenders. The defender who is called out must box out the shooter.

The other 3 defenders must communicate to each other which offensive player they're going to box out.

The goal for the defensive team is to secure the rebound.

Scoring System:
There are a couple of ways you can score this drill:

- Set a number of defensive rebounds the defensive team must get before the teams switch over. Three is usually a good amount.
- Get 3 consecutive defensive rebounds in a row. Made shots don't end the streak, only offensive rebounds.

Coaching Points:

- Defenders must touch the outsides of the key when they're sliding. Coaches should be alert to the correct move of the legs in the slides.

- Be sure the defenders are putting in the effort with their slides. Nothing half-hearted. Refuse to pass the ball to the offensive team until they're going hard.
- The offensive team must be ready to shoot when they receive the ball.
- Stutter the feet on the close-out. No jumping.

ROTATION REBOUNDING (EARLY AND MID-SEASON)

This drill involves an even number of either 3 or 4 players rotating around the key. The offensive team is rotating clockwise, and the defensive team is rotating counterclockwise. When the coach shoots the basketball, the defenders must quickly find an offensive player to box out before securing the rebound. The drill then leads into a game of 3-on-3 or 4-on-4 with one score or one stop the goal.

Purpose:
A fun rebounding drill variation that emphasizes the importance of defenders communicating, working as a team, and making contact with an offensive player before securing the rebound.

Setup:
- 4 players on offense. 2 on the low blocks and 2 on the elbows.
- 4 defenders on the inside of each of the offensive players.
- The rest of the players are behind the baseline.
- Coach stands on the free throw line with a basketball.

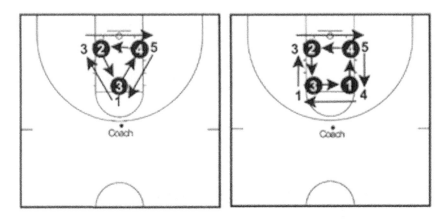

The coach begins the drill by calling out "Start" or "Go" to the players.

The 3 defenders start rotating counterclockwise around the key on the inside of the offensive players in a low stance.

The 3 offensive players start rotating clockwise around the key on the outside of the defensive players in a correct defensive stance.

After a short amount of time, the coach attempts a shot from the free throw line. As soon as the shot is in the air, the players react and battle to secure the rebound. NOTE: using a manager for the shooting assists the coach to observe and correct the techniques of the players more clearly.

If the defenders get the rebound, the drill transitions up and down the floor in 4-on-4 with both teams playing both offense and defense.

If the offensive team gets the rebound, the play is live. They must attempt to score at the same end of the floor.

Variations:

3-on-3 or 4-on-4 The drill can be run with teams of either 3 or 4 players. If there are teams of 3, the starting formation is a triangle. If there are teams of 4, the starting formation is a square.

No Transition—It's not compulsory to transition up and back off the rebound. You can simply use this as a rebounding drill and then set up again.

Coaching Points:

It's important that the defenders talk to each other throughout the rotations at the start of the drill. They must know who's going to box out whom on a shot attempt.

The defenders should be making contact and not allowing the offensive players to move closer to the rim after the shot.

On a defensive rebound, the offensive team should push the basketball down the floor before the defense sets up.

Players must jump with two hands for every rebound.

Players must quickly get into an outlet position after a rebound so that the transition from defense to offense can be done quickly.

WEAKSIDE REBOUNDING

Two offensive players are located on the wing and corner outside the arc. Two defenders are in the weakside positions near the split-line. The coach has a basketball on the opposite wing. The coach shoots the basketball and the two defenders must box out the offensive players and secure the offensive rebound.

Purpose:

Many players have a habit of lacking the necessary concentration about boxing out when they're in help positions, so this drill gets players used to boxing out from the weakside spots. This drill focuses on players' finding their assignments, going to get them, and then making and keeping the contact after the coach shoots. At that point it is a matter of getting the ball.

Setup:

- Offensive players are positioned on the wing and corner outside the arc.
- Defensive players (x1 and x2) are positioned in the correct help spots.
- The rest of the players form two lines with one defender behind each offensive player.
- Coach has a basketball.

The coach begins the drill by shooting the basketball while the defenders are in correct help positions. The coach shoots to miss, but any make is treated as a miss.

The offensive players (1 and 2) both crash the boards looking to secure an offensive rebound.

The defensive players (x1 and x2) must leave their help position, find and make contact with the offensive players they're guarding, and then pursue the defensive rebound.

If the defense secures the rebound, they are rewarded by staying on defense while the offensive players rotate out, and two new players play offense.

If the offensive team secures the rebound, they switch to defense for the next repetition, and the current defensive players rotate out to the end of the line with a new set of offensive players coming in.

Scoring System:

The drill is scored individually on how many defensive rebounds each player gets.

- Any time a player secures a defensive rebound, both defensive players receive a point.

- There are no points awarded for an offensive rebound.

- At the end of the drill, whichever player has the most points wins.

Coaching Points:

Players must pursue the basketball until one of the teams secures it. The offensive team should make every effort to get the ball, even if they knock it out of bounds. Defenders are only awarded points if they secure the defensive rebound while in bounds.

Start your defenders in the help positions that you emphasize with your defense. Some coaches have the players helping from the split-line (the imaginary line that runs down the middle of the floor from baseline to baseline) and others start them on the edge of the key.

Players must alternate lines, so they get repetitions from both the wing and the corner.

Defenders must seek contact and be the first one to initiate contact on the box out. Forearm contact should precede the pivot to the actual box out. The pivot and actual box out resemble a strong post position: legs wide and in mid-center, arms high.

Make sure the defenders stay in mid-stance and can always see their assignment and the ball. If the players cheat to the weak side or lose vision of the ball, the coach dribbles toward the basket. The defender finds the ball and secures the box out.

Remind your players about the importance of boxing out in this position. Frequently, a rebound is made on the opposite side of where the shot came from.

The three drills, Rotation Rebounding, Slide Rebounding, and Weak Side Rebounding are courtesy of www.basketballforcoaches.com/rebounding-drills/

COACH McCORMACK'S COMPETITIVE 3-PLAYER REBOUNDING DRILL

Three or more players and one ball are required for this drill. Two players locate just outside the arc, one at each free-throw line extended, and one player located directly under the rim. One of the players outside the arc will have the ball in triple threat position. Any extra players line up behind each other, behind the baseline and even with the basket.

1. The drill starts with a pass from the player on the arc with the ball, across the lane to the other player on the arc, who catches and immediately shoots a 3-point shot.

2. The player under the rim takes a step toward the pass receiver, in a stance pointing to and seeing both the shooter and passer.

3. On the shot, the player that passed the ball becomes an offensive rebounder, and the defender in the lane is the defensive rebounder. The shot is played as a miss by both whether the shot is made or not.

4. Now the battle is on! Whichever player gets the rebound immediately passes out to the player who just shot and sprints out to become the next shooter from the arc.

Coaching Points:

Any time the ball goes out of bounds, no matter who lost it, it is a repeat. This assures maximum and multiple efforts from the offensive rebounder and requires the defensive rebounder to not only block out, but also locate and get the ball. Most misses will rebound long from the basket, requiring the defender to position away from the rim to execute an effective block-out (usually outside the lane to be effective).

We suggest two minutes for the drill with 3 players, and three minutes with 4 or 5 players. Score 1 pt. for a defensive rebound, 1 pt. for a made shot, and 2 points for an offensive rebound. Players must call out their totals on every score.

Besides the points, the reward for getting an offensive or defensive rebound is becoming the next shooter and then offensive rebounder for more possible points. However, to get or stay on offense requires a rebound first.

If there are more than 3 players in the drill, the player who does not get the rebound steps out of bounds under the basket. The next player waiting out of bounds then steps in to be the next defensive rebounder.

The losers at the end of the time limit have to do 10 pushups or sit-ups. The winner shoots a free-throw; if made, he/she counts the reps for the losers. If missed, he/she also does the reps.

This drill develops skill, toughness and stamina. Coaches running the drill must be very vocal and energetic. Players who get stuck on defense or out of bounds for more than a couple shots need to take it personally.

If you are doing this drill in groups, balance the groups. A suggestion is the next time you do the drill, match up the winners.

And another favorite…

REPEATED QUICK JUMP DRILL

This drill emphasizes the importance of the 2nd and 3rd jump to secure the board.

Players are under the basket in front of the rim. They must jump and touch the rim or as high as they can jump three times with left hand; three times right; three times with both hands.

Key Point:
They cannot gather themselves after each jump; they must hit the floor and go right up nine times in a row.

Add yet another favorite…

BO RYAN 2 ON 2 CLOSEOUT/BLOCK OUT REBOUNDING DRILL

The object of the drill is to get two defensive rebounds (stops) in a row to go on offense. If the offense scores or gets an offensive rebound, the defense goes back to zero. The main defensive skills are:

- Closing out with urgency and under control with proper hand and foot technique.

- Contest to block out technique on a shooter: Avoid contact with the shooter until that player takes a step after landing. Fouling a jump shooter is never acceptable.

- Moving from the help position to the correct block out technique off the ball.
- Sprinting for the ball.
- Yelling, "Shot!" on a shot attempt for good communication.
- The defense must secure the rebound before it goes out of bounds.

The main offensive skills involved are:

- Offensive rebounding mind set and techniques
- Shot ready and triple threat on the catch
- Holding the follow through and concentration on the 3-point shot
- Maximizing the dribble

The drill starts with a coach with a ball just above the 3-point arc at the top of the key. Two defensive players stand on the free throw line, touching fists in the middle and facing the coach. Two players are on offense, standing just outside the 3-point arc at the free throw line extended in a catch-and-shoot stance.

The coach passes to either offensive player who has two choices: 1) Shoot a 3-point shot, or 2) Shot fake and drive to the basket with a one dribble limit to a finish or a kick-out pass.

The defender on the ball side closes out under control and takes away the rhythm release point of the shooter without fouling. Coaches must be alert for fouls on shooters; those fouls are purposeless and hurt defenses. Players cannot foul jump shooters!

The defender on the help line must get to the mid-line first—with one foot over the mid-line—to help on any drive and recover. A drive and kick to the opposite wing might require communication for a switch. Also, the offensive players may only go to the offensive board from outside the lane and not until the shot is released. Again, coaches should call any violation. A player who penetrates and passes to a teammate or the coach must sprint back outside the 3-point arc before going to the board.

On any pass to a coach at the top of the key, the drill goes back to the starting position, but the coach does not wait for the defenders. They must touch fists in the middle before closing out.

On any made shot or offensive rebound, the ball is passed back to the coach, but the action does not stop after an offensive rebound.

We allow a maximum of two passes before a shot attempt, even if a shot has to be forced. We want a high volume of shots quickly. The coach can also incorporate a pass fake and reverse or return pass to the wings. The players should be the shooters, but every once in a while, the coach may shoot for a change of pace. If a player makes a shot, the action is reset, and the defense goes to zero. If a coach shoots, since he/she is not guarded or contested, the action continues. Make or miss until a rebound is secured or the ball goes out of bounds. If the offense scores or gets the offensive rebound, the defense goes to zero.

Because the main skills emphasized are closeouts and block outs, you may want to introduce the drill without the driving option or the coach shooting until the basic points of emphasis are applied.

If the ball goes out of bounds, even off the offense, the defense does not go back to zero, but no stop is awarded. This guideline keeps the offensive players going to the boards hard.

The drill turns into a nice shooting drill, too. It also develops resilience and mental and physical toughness. Imagine working on defense through several tough possessions having one stop and then having to start over due to a missed close out, boxout, or failure to help. Sometimes the defense does everything great and the offense still scores. Guess what? That's part of the highs and lows of this great game.

Putting the better players with the weaker ones is a great way to keep the better players working hard. Sometimes, it's very interesting when we let players choose their partners for the drill. The choices send a pretty good message because players will pick according to the level of their teammates' competitive toughness.

Where opposing mentalities contrast...

DEFENSIVE REBOUNDING

Find the target first.

- Try to be outside the rim for the rebound.

- The longer the shot, the longer the rebound.

- For shots from the corners by the opponent, the middle of the lane must be controlled for defensive rebounds.

- One of the most difficult accomplishments on defense is being able to allow only one shot by the opponent in a fast break or transition situation. So often, second shots from a missed layup are critical moments in losses for that defense. Fouls mount and key possessions are gained or lost.

- It is less important that a certain player gets the rebound from a missed shot; it is vastly more important that any one of the defenders gets the rebound.

- Rebounding becomes a disadvantage by players' thinking they can just outjump their opponents. In some cases, outjumping works. However, as the game progresses and fatigue sets in, position for rebounding on defense is the bottom line. Always look for the opponent first, make contact, establish block out position, and find the ball. Then sprint and/or jump for the ball. Rebounders should come down with the ball with legs spread and, if possible, facing the sideline to start a break.

OFFENSIVE REBOUNDING

Find the ball first. Players have to practice that move. Finding the ball while simultaneously getting position is a true skill.

- Love the contact. Get the early position.

- Offensive rebounders should get their elbows and hands higher than the defenders' elbows. Fingers "to the sky."

- If position is earned early, a firm seal must follow.

- Knowing teammates' shooting tendencies well, the good offensive rebounder can anticipate the move for inside position.

- Keeping the ball alive and/or tipping the missed shot to oneself is an instinctive, excellent way to retain possession.

- Rebounding becomes a disadvantage by players' thinking they can just outjump the opponent. Sometimes the quick jump helps keep a ball alive for a teammate. Overall, though, early position with a wide stance and the eyes on the ball are the foundations for good offensive rebounding.

- Last shot of the game: Design a play based on offensive rebounding position. Many games are won on the put-back rather than the first shot. This design is against both man and zone defenses. If a free throw needs to be missed, use a cross screen by one player so that the teammate can get hands on the miss to tap the ball back out to the foul shooter who has back stepped behind a back screen by a teammate outside the arc.

Against good box out teams, the following three techniques are effective but must be instructed well and practiced:

- A spin and seal move or counter step, which is used against a defender who blocks out well.

- A dive to hook the arm with a whip with the inside leg around the opponent is effective on free throw rebounding.

- Step back and around.

"Rebounding is the most underrated concept in victory. Rebounding is 25 percent ability and 75 percent attitude."

~George Raveling

A – ATTENTIVENESS

"Listening is never casual."

~Bill Russell

"I told players to relax and never to think about what's at stake, just the basketball game. If you start to think about who's going to win the championship, you've lost your focus."

~Michael Jordan
Chicago Bulls

MAY WE HAVE YOUR ATTENTION?

This chapter might be one of the shortest ones in this book, but it is one of the most vital. Why not get your cold one now before starting to read?

 REFLECTION

TOM McCORMACK

Coach Bruce Hildabrand, a longtime assistant in the Conant program and close friend, told a great analogy to players about the comparison between the attention required to driving a car with the development of basketball individual and team skills. Getting a driver's license and the car keys are big deals to high school players. Starting the demonstration with that topic was an instant attention getter. He then described that in both driving and basketball, the development of the student-athlete starts out slowly, learning and practicing the required performance skills. As proficiency increases, so do speed and the degree of difficulty.

Anticipation and reaction time become vital components of the student-athlete's readiness to drive in real traffic. Knowing where the gas and brake pedals are located and how to apply them are of equal importance. With enough time and practice, the student-athlete graduates to the fast lane where decisions are made not in seconds, but in milliseconds. We equated trust in a player as the equivalent to giving them the car keys with the responsibilities that go with them. They were not handed out easily and came with strings attached. Stay in your lane (perform your role), few to no accidents (execution errors), and no speeding or parking tickets (turnovers). Attention to the details of skill and team execution needs to graduate from a thought process to one that anticipates and reacts correctly in those milliseconds.

A side note to you coaches who are now or will become parents. My wife and I established with our four children a rule that worked out very well in our home. This rule applied to both driving and extra-curricular activities:

At least all Bs or no car keys.

A short and strict probationary period usually followed with mandatory remediation for any violators. We did not have many second offenders.

POINTS TO PONDER

Why is attentiveness so instrumental for a quality program?

- Attentiveness is non-negotiable. Without this behavior, any potential for a great program will fall by the wayside. Attentiveness is never a request; it is a demand from all involved, from head coach to player, player to coaches, coaches to coaches, etc. Attentiveness is a mindset, an attitude conducive to constant improvement. Attentiveness is ongoing and once established, should take on a life of its own as a program staple and a daily part of living. "God gave us two ears and one tongue."

- We believe eye contact remains a fundamental component for attentiveness. Without it, the establishment of good relationships is difficult to build and to sustain. Once eye contact is established as a daily habit, better communication has a chance to happen. For us, the eyes had to be visible before any constructive criticism, instruction, or discussion occurred. This demand was consistent throughout our programs: in practices, scouting, timeouts, arguments, or friendly banter. Good eye contact is a starter for player improvement; coaches need to use it, too. Eyes convey feelings and levels of trust; on the other hand, the lack of eyes indicates problems which must be fixed before they fester. Eye contact is a plus for thorough attentiveness.

- Coach John Wooden stated this priority in different words, "If you don't take the time to do it right, then you better make the time to do it over." Correct repetition does have its time and place, but why waste time in lieu of attentiveness?

- Attentiveness begins with the instruction of sound fundamentals to which good listening belongs. To reaffirm that statement, read the following anecdote by Lou Holtz, former head football coach at the University of Notre Dame:

THE IMPORTANCE OF FUNDAMENTALS

A man walked into a pet store to buy a bird. He settled on one that cost $1.95 and went to pay. The proprietor said to him, "Why settle for that one when I can show you a bird that sings and talks?" The man said okay so the owner showed him that bird which cost $621.

Curious and eager, the man brought the bird home, but on the following day, brought it back to the pet shop, and said, "This bird doesn't do a thing; I never heard any singing or talking. I want my money back."

The owner said, "What did the bird do when you rang the bell? Did you buy the bell? It needs the bell to do the singing and talking. It's only $11."

The next day the man returned, complaining again that there was no singing or talking.

The store owner said, "Sir, that's impossible. I have the same bird as you. Just this morning, my bird got up and ran up the ladder…"

The startled customer said, "What ladder?"

"The bird won't talk or sing unless you have the ladder and it's only $16," said the owner.

Satisfied, the man went home with the ladder for the bird.

This went on for four days, and each day the owner sold the man something.

After four more days, the man returned to the pet shop and said, "I invested $727 in that bird and today my bird finally talked to me just before he died. He climbed the ladder, rang the bell, swung on his swing, poked the mirror, and his last and only words were, "Didn't he sell ya any bird seed?"

See what we mean?
The importance of fundamentals.

Coaches Attend to Matters Such As:

- Teaching the importance and techniques for listening by the players which begin and end with eye contact
- Evaluating the results of eye contact which are communication, understanding, improvement, coordination of the fundamentals and various parts of the game with precise execution

- Determining if a player is "varsity-ready" which is an underlying baseline for all player development, feeder through high school

- Establishing that learning and improvement are specific aims that lead to winning

- Supplying clear directions during instruction of techniques and skills

- Determining the suitability and timing of players' questions

- Knowing that in some players' cultural backgrounds, eye contact can be interpreted as a sign of confrontation or a lack of respect, so with those players more patience and understanding are necessary to develop positive eye contact

- Keeping clear communication among staff regarding personnel decisions where input is valued, but once a decision is made, everyone is on board

- Demonstrating the skill to keep players' attention through good organization of practices and application of details in each skill that makes players and teams better

- Demonstrating the ability to keep the team focused despite distractions, the media, and other outside influences

- Knowing what skills, principles, particular defense, and offensive movements apply for each season

- Determining which five players make the best team, not necessarily the group with the five best players

- Acknowledging and motivating every player on the team, one through fifteen

- Creating the right physical spacing in game timeouts so that true attentiveness is gained

- Gaining the attention of players at practice or in a game, such as a whistle, along with a clear understanding of what the immediate expectation is

 REFLECTION

TOM McCORMACK

I never used a whistle at practice. I had the ability to whistle quite loudly on my own without the use of a manufactured one. This also enabled me to use my whistle in games to get the players' attention. When I watch a team at practice, I am always interested what happens immediately after the whistle blows. Are there any more shots or dribbles? Do heads turn immediately? Is the immediate response urgent or casual? Our expectation was one of immediate attention and reaction or.... My four adult children still react with a quick head turn to that whistle today, although without quite the same sense of urgency.

- Being smart and responsible in setting up the schedules for both practices and games...Don't leave those items up to the athletic director. The working relationship between the head coach and the athletic director is of major importance. Trust in each other and competence in each's respective jobs are the major ingredients that go into making the relationship productive for both the individual program and the athletic department as a whole. As a rule, neither party likes to be surprised, especially by things that can be communicated ahead of time. We have each worked with several A.D.s during our careers, each with his or her own unique personality and way of doing things. Make it a point to find out what the specific expectations are from each other. There are issues that can be compromised or delegated and those that cannot. Make it a point to be clear on these issues. A weekly sit down together to go over athletic issues or just shoot the breeze goes a long way towards keeping the relationship friendly and productive for everyone. Three other questions to know the answers: 1) *Who hired you?* 2) *Who can fire you?*

3) *Who is the boss?* Always remember it is more productive to work with someone, rather than for someone.

- Taking good care of those quiet heroes, those unsung heroes who can make or break your program and its image: front office and athletic secretaries, trainers, custodians, etc. Keeping friendly relationships with those people, even surprising them with team t-shirts or birthday gifts can go a long way for sustaining a positive vibe about your program with the general public.

- Adapting, an asset coaches must develop in the long term, in the short term, and in the spur of the moment-three different scenarios, but all guaranteed to occur over the course of one's coaching career. Actually, all three may occur during the course of a single season or even less. Spur of the moment ones are usually quick, game time decisions that hopefully have been prepared in practice. For example, the opponent changes to a box-and-one defense after a timeout. Experience is the best teacher here. Short term ones are usually the type that a coach may have a little time to prepare for. When a coach is in tournament play and the opponent who he/she plans to play in the next game loses, there is a scramble to prepare for a completely different opponent in less than a day. Quality assistants and thorough scouting reports are extremely helpful here. Long term ones are major adjustments that require diligent research, preparation, and practice. Some examples of these are the 3-point shot, the Elam Ending, playing 18-minute halves instead of four 8-minute quarters in high school varsity games. Then there is the current debate of a shot clock, now in some states and possibly soon added in others. These types require adjustments primarily in defensive and offensive strategy and team play, but the commitment to developing the Big 3 in the Big Ten remains the basic core of player development.

A suggestion regarding long-term decisions: If you have an opinion or a voice in any long-term decisions affecting your program or the game itself, express your opinion to the right people in the appropriate manner. Don't let others speak for you. Informed leadership is required in critical decisions, and sometimes the person or committee with the decision-making authority is not the expert. You as the coach are.

- Attending to the feeder programs: Until a coach is actually a head coach, a factor not really understood is the full range of responsibilities. In addition to the list in the Preparation section, the head coach also has the responsibility of developing the progression of the feeder level programs. This progression includes fundamental and advanced teaching of skills and implementing the offensive and defensive structures and philosophy. The following are some pointers in developing the attentiveness necessary for these areas:

Be specific with the coaches at these levels about the skills taught and the instruction of them. Coaches' meetings, clinics, and player camps are helpful here, especially for the youngest groups. Some programs use the same offensive and defensive sets from the youngest levels, possibly 3rd or 4th grade, through the varsity level. Others have a progression. For example, we used a Flex offense and man-to-man defense with our feeder and freshman levels, so all players played in the post and on the perimeter. After freshman year we began to specialize and tailor our offensive and defensive sets around the players' specific talents and skills. Even though philosophies vary on the types of skills, sets, and progressions, and at the level to introduce them, the most important point is to have a philosophy with a plan to implement it. Former players can be prime candidates to coach the feeder programs. If possible, pay feeder level coaches a modest stipend, and put a reliable person in charge of directing the feeder program. The director needs to be trustworthy and loyal to the head coach and to the program's philosophy. Having the right person in this important position can not only be a positive force for the whole program, but also save the head coach a lot of headaches. Many high school and feeder players today also play for other teams out of season. Try to get a feel for what is being taught and what these players are bringing back with them, both good and bad. This can have a wide influence on their progress. Make yourself available to these outside team's coaches and programs to explore ways of cooperation. A word of caution here: It is important to hear what they say, but more important to watch what they do. Stay alert and never let your program be sabotaged. Keep parents in the loop, including recommendations for off-season teams and trainers. You recommend them, not the other way around. Delegate some of these duties to assistant coaches but oversee their work.

Coaches Encourage and Push Players to be Attentive To:

- Keeping themselves organized: family-school-basketball-social life.

- Learning how to listen well with consistent eye contact, then doing it all the time, even if they are having a bad day, a bad practice, or feeling ill.

- Getting enough sleep, eating right, dressing appropriately, being a good example in all areas.

- Executing the key details and fundamentals for application of all skills.

- Learning to bracket distractions: Bracketing temporarily sets aside personal prejudices, distractions, and desires so the listener can experience as far as possible the speaker's message.

- Making good friends and good choices.

- Keeping positive relationships with teammates.

- Applying the cerebral nature of basketball to improve their ability to play the game well within the team concept.

- Becoming an example of pride, hard work, and selflessness in the classroom, hallways, cafeteria, and court.

- Making the program's traditions handed down from team to team over the years to become standards of pride and kept with diligence and integrity. Traditions can never be allowed to cross the line to hazing, bullying, or exclusiveness. Those unacceptable actions must be addressed in oral and written directives during pre-season meetings with parents and players.

 REFLECTION

TOM McCORMACK

Goal setting for teams and individual players is a prime factor for attentiveness. We set performance goals for individuals and for teams, rather than a certain number of wins. The Green Light Shirt award was one goal for individuals. One distinction that we established for the team was the program's all-time history listed on the back of our warm-up shirts every season. A goal for each of our teams became to achieve something for the back of the shirt that that team could add to the Cougar tradition. That achievement passed on as a challenge to the teams that followed.

Conant warm-up shirt   Conant "Green Light" shirt

FACTORS ASSISTING ATTENTIVENESS

When all is said and done, coaches try to teach and instill the reactive, "muscle-memory" habits that result from correct decisions made in fractions of seconds. We as coaches tend to be laser focused when introducing a fundamental concept or team strategy. As teachers we also need to be keenly aware if we are getting through to our student learners. This might require more volume, better eye contact, a less distractive location, or a different approach entirely. When teaching the skills of the game as well as possible with maximum attention from players, coaches should consider and prepare:

- an atmosphere conducive to quality instruction
- the use of necessary wait-time that encourages attention from all listeners
- a good plan so that a new drill is taught early in practices when players are fresher
- eye contact to each player as instruction unfolds
- sufficient volume so that every player can hear clearly
- clear goals for the instruction, explaining why we are doing this particular movement or drill
- the use of the best demonstrators

- a logical breakdown of the instructed action: "See it; try it; rein-struct; try it again; enfold into the mainstream of the offense or defense." If the drill is essential to teach one day, bring it back the next day, and forever after.

The Explanation and Demonstration Method for Skill Instruction

Often, the first time the skills such as the "Big 3" are introduced to players is in a summer camp or clinic. One overarching goal is to establish and ingrain these habits so that during the season they just need polishing, not reteaching. Teaching and re-teaching skills are appropriate, usually necessary, at the lower levels but cut into team time at the varsity level.

The Proficiency and Skill of the Instructor

The proficiency and skill of the instructor is the next step. Rarely try to demonstrate a skill you cannot perform well. Faking the skill is not a good idea. Players see right through this tomfoolery; thus, the demonstrator's credibility loses respect. In many cases where the coach tries to demonstrate and cannot, the players lose whatever level of attentiveness with which they began. Only have coaches, players, or possibly alumni who are masters of the skill demonstrate. An excellent way to teach a skill for coaches who are not great at it themselves is to explain the components of the skill while someone proficient is performing it. Videos can be a useful tool. If coaches are the actual demonstrators, they should make sure they first command the group's attention. Telling a story of a past player who passed or dribbled well, a personal story from the coach's playing career, or a relevant tale from a famous alumnus raises the interest of the listeners and their eye contact. Plus, stories promote silence. Asking or hiring a specialist to demonstrate a particular skill is helpful, if budgets allow. Most coaches have areas they are very proficient in and some they are not. The good ones know the difference and are not afraid or too intimidated to ask for help. A great example of this type of coaching relationship was the Marquette University staff in the 1970's with head coach Al McGuire and his assistants Hank Raymonds and Rick Majerus. Al recruited and motivated; Hank supplied the offensive philosophy and plays; Rick mastered and taught the defense and worked closely with the players. They were three very different personalities with skill sets that blended very effectively.

The Primary Learning Style(s) of the Players

This area is a prime aspect of attentiveness and involves coaches' knowing the personalities of the players as well as possible. Certainly, players would rather practice a skill than watch it. Know your audience. Try to implement a variety of learning tools: kinetic, auditory, visual, or suitable combinations. Having players visualize (discussed in Mentality) the skill quietly before they try it and after they practice it can be effective. Visualization is a form of acute attention.

Let's use teaching shooting mechanics as an example. There are several theories here. Action steps like foot placement, knee bend and leg lift, trunk rotation and alignment, hand placement, ball on body location, ball dip, elbow alignment and lift, placement of non-shooting hand, shoulder alignment, head position and sight line to target, release point, body angles start to finish, release, follow through and ball rotation, fluid momentum or hesitation stop, pushing vs. throwing motion, landing, etc. are all teaching points that require attention to detail. Those parts make up the whole. Suffice it to say, arriving at a consistent release point for each shot is a common goal.

The Size and Range of the Group to be Instructed

The aforementioned teaching points about shooting mechanics are a lot for players to digest. The more individual attention given the better, so keeping groups small (fewer than ten per coach, if possible) will help focus both the coach and those particular players. A recommendation for group instruction is to use the "whole-part-whole" method. The instructor demonstrates the whole shot and gets the group's attention. From that point, the coach features a certain aspect for correct shooting, foot placement and leg power, for example. Then, groups work with assistants who actively monitor the group with intervals of demonstration breaking down the specific individual mechanic just emphasized and build the shot layer by layer. Another way is to bring in the groups again and again to emphasize a certain part of the shot or skill being taught, then going to baskets to concentrate on that particular piece of the puzzle. We recommend taking the basket out of the drill work for the players until the entire shot is in place, and even then, not until you are satisfied with their attention to detail and execution of the parts. At some point they must actually shoot. Start players in front of the rim, moving them out two steps after a certain number of repetitions. Most of the work needed to be done is on their own or with a partner. We all desire the end result of a high percentage shot, but in the initial phases, praise proper mechanics and not the end results. Whatever technique for instruction coaches might select, they should not lecture for more than ten minutes. Players' minds wander after that amount of time and any more instruction loses its impact. Thus, coaches need to prepare their teaching to insure maximum concentration from their charges. It is the hope that each subsequent day's instruction builds upon what was taught the previous day. Coaches need to ask, "Where do I want these players, dependent upon their ages and abilities, to be by the end of the week or the month?" Coaches also need to be ready to adjust and avoid moving on too quickly.

The Facilities and Equipment Available with Some Creativity

The gym or outdoor space and the number of baskets and basketballs need planning. For example, with a small group of ten, the desire is to have five basketballs so that players can work with a partner. Perhaps only two basketballs are available. Two lines of five are sustainable, although not the best option. If younger players are not directly involved with action, attention suffers. The same principle might also apply to varsity players. Much is dependent on the maturity levels of the individuals, another factor for coaches to consider when planning instruction with facilities in mind. Many of these responsibilities can be shared or delegated. No task is beneath any person in the program, including the head coach.

Each of the above factors plays a role in determining the attentiveness and the attention to detail that needs to be put into all the various skills involved in the game. Coaches, if you want attention back, you must put attention in. It is also desirable to have assistants on the staff with a diversity of skills such as team play, skill instruction, skill demonstration, technology, scouting, and many of the areas identified in the Preparation chapter.

The attentiveness demanded in communication and teaching or learning the game are the critical bonds the coach and the players must share to build the team. Attentiveness is not a request. It is a necessary component for total team preparation with the required professional instruction in the details toward ultimate victory.

 REFLECTION

TOM McCORMACK

As coaches we were always looking for ways to improve our program. At Conant we had just finished the 1988-89 season, the breakthrough for our program. After having a 2-48 record the first two years, that season contained lots of progress with a 15-12 mark. We had a great court and three other gyms for practice, but with all our levels and the other winter sports like girls' basketball, cheerleading, etc. sharing the same spaces, having a somewhat constant practice routine with minimal distractions was impossible. Having a later practice time in the evening usually meant a prime space with fewer distractions, but the tradeoff was study and family time.

In the early '80s our Immaculate Conception High School basketball staff with Tom Anstett as the head coach, attended a clinic where John Chaney from Temple University spoke. His topic was the matchup zone, his team's trademark. During his presentation he also talked about the benefits of morning practice. 5:30 a.m. was their standard practice time. Of the many benefits he listed about morning practice, the ones that stood out in my mind were the steady routine that allowed for family and study time and the exclusive use of the main gym. That time provided minimal distractions and a quiet atmosphere for good teaching and listening. Good attentiveness from all parties led to precise instruction, closer attention from the audience, and less repetition. After some deliberation with my staff-who believed I was insane-our athletic director agreed and helped me convince the principal. We started 5:30 to 7:45 a.m. practices which we continued for the next 29 years until I retired. The new head coach still uses that system.

The results testify that it worked well for our program. Except after a weeknight game, we practiced early and held open gyms early for the same reasons. It became part of "the Cougar Way" and a matter of pride for our program's players and coaches.

Our players loved it when other programs' players told us we were nuts, but when someone might tell you you're crazy, you know you're getting somewhere. For our family, my wife, our four children, and myself, the benefits were tremendous. I was able to be home a lot more and see many of my kids' events I might have otherwise missed. I'd like to add to the married coaches: having a supportive spouse and family is paramount to success. Not being able to coordinate family life and coaching demands is one of the main reasons good coaches leave coaching far too early in their teaching careers.

I am not saying morning practice works for everyone because facilities, administrations, and family situations vary, but this change is something for head coaches to ponder. Perhaps consider it during your next practice when you cannot hear yourself think, or the players cannot hear what you are instructing due to the various noises that envelope the gym.

 REFLECTION

TOM ANSTETT

When I was an English department chairman, I observed many teachers in their classroom instruction. I witnessed some teachers trying to talk over the noise from their students, repeating directions all too often, or becoming frustrated at students' lack of attention. Many of these situations were eventually solved through better patience, better preparation, and eye contact. Such "little things" once achieved made all the difference in lowering those teachers' frustration levels and increasing their confidence and instruction. Better relationships ensued.

On the court, I demanded eye contact no matter what the situation. I especially wanted a player's eyes when we had disagreements. Those situations were never easy but offered benefits for all involved. Players learned to accept criticism, no matter the level of intensity from the excitable coach. Being 6'7" was an obstacle at times. Players and students were timid in my presence, so communication was a challenge. I had the habit of standing a lot on the sidelines, but as my career progressed, I sat more so the coach and the player could see eye to eye for clearer communication. In time, I learned to think more before I said something I might regret. In any event, eye contact was always maintained because it is necessary for any quality relationship.

In *The Last Dance*, the 2020 ESPN documentary featuring the Chicago Bulls' dynasty in the 1990s, there is a moment captured in the second episode between general manager Jerry Krause and star player Scottie Pippen. Krause is talking to Pippen who seems to be fixing his belt as he dresses. Pippen's head is down and his eyes distant from Krause. Perhaps there is no better snapshot of the poor relationship between those two important pieces in the Bulls' championship years. Pippen refuses to give his attention to Krause; Krause refuses to wait for Pippen to look at him. This episode stands in stark contrast to the esteemed late football and baseball coach at the University of St. Francis, Gordon Gillespie. When Gordie needed his players' attention, his expression was, "Give me your eyes." Then, he waited until that decree was fulfilled.

The eyes have it.

"It's the little details that are vital.
Little things make big things happen."

~John Wooden
UCLA

M – MENTALITY

"The greatest sin a coach can commit is to allow kids to slide by.
This goes for the classroom as well as the court."

~Hubie Brown
Former NBA Coach, Current Analyst

"I step on the court. That's me.
I don't play around.
I'm not there to be your best friend."

~Kobe Bryant
Los Angeles Lakers

"To win the big games, you must get to the free throw line,
and then you must make them."

~Rick Majerus
Marquette University, University of Utah, St. Louis University

"You're either getting better or getting worse.
You never stay the same."

~Ray Meyer
DePaul University Blue Demons

POINTS TO PONDER

Pat Riley played basketball at the University of Kentucky, then for two NBA teams, and won several NBA championships as a coach. He was the youngest of three brothers. When he was young, Pat was often excluded from neighborhood pick-up games. One day his father came home and found Pat crying because he couldn't play and was pushed around by the older boys. His father said, "Every now and then, there comes a day when some place, some time, you simply have to plant your feet, stand firm, and make a statement about who you are and what you believe in." (paraphrased from The Winner Within)

The Pat Riley anecdote introduces the challenge of attaining mental toughness. How and when does an athlete hurdle the tendency of all human nature of taking the easy way out? William Faulkner, the great American novelist, believed that courage is the most essential quality a person can exhibit. He said, "You cannot swim for new horizons until you have the courage to lose sight of the shore." Within those two examples lie the three steps for the mentality necessary for mental toughness: 1. Know the problem. 2. Know how to fix it. 3. Fix it. It is in the third step where too many coaches and athletes fall short. Most of the time, that wall of self-defeat materializes through faulty comparisons with others' performances. Instead, coaches and players should confront the standards and expectations they have for themselves and evaluate honestly where they are. Are they setting challenging goals? Where are they in terms of accomplishing those goals? What kind of work is being put into attaining the goals? Many coaches and athletes want to improve but lack the planning for growth in order to improve. For example, if players are asked what their goals are before a certain game, most will predictably say, "Win." Players with plans might reply, "Use my dribble more efficiently," or "Rebound better on the offensive end." Those specific goals lead to winning. Those specific replies suggest a mindset for growth that must be taught and practiced by coaches.

Thus, as a frame of reference for this chapter, mentality means "a collective mindset for growth." We like this definition for two reasons: first, the word "collective" reinforces the true team concept within basketball; and second, "mindset for growth" suggests the various ways coaches can empower their young players to advance physically, mentally, socially, and emotionally. Everything we describe and explain in this chapter underscores this definition.

The following illustrates one aspect of how this growth mindset can manifest in a basketball program. Competing, winning, and playing time form a tightrope that coaches must walk to attain and keep their teams playing hard, smart, and together. It's a beautiful thing when these three ideals align. A long season is usually in store when they do not.

Consider this idea for a moment. How does a coach communicate the mentality of unselfishness and overachievement to the team? Some teams struggle to share the ball, reverse the ball, hunt for a great shot, pass into the post, etc. When teams don't share the ball, confusion, lack of spacing, lack of screening or movement, lack of passing, and lack of trust ensue. A similar case occurs at the other end of the floor when players do not communicate on defense.

There are only two possible reasons for a team's mental state when these things occur, selfishness or ignorance. Ignorance is easier to fix than selfishness. An education of observing, explaining, conditioning, and drilling cure ignorance in most cases. With time and repetition, players will respond well because the majority are willing learners.

With selfish players, explaining the flaw in their attitude in hopes they will change their behavior is worth a try, but unfortunately that effort can be quite frustrating and perhaps unsuccessful. Coach Bob Huggins at the University of West Virginia has a simple process to solve this problem. It's called "run and sit," meaning a player will run or not play until the attitude and action are acceptable. These players usually understand that basic principle and then have to make a decision. Some decide wisely and fold back into the program's mentality. However, some get lost in themselves, and it's a tough road back if they do not change. Understanding the how of "run and sit" is basic but understanding the why is necessary for the selfish player to convert to the team-oriented system of play.

Before the time players reach the varsity, it is critical for coaches to know what type of education players need to grow and compete. The first type is fun for both the players and coach when the light bulbs go on and progress happens. The second type can be rewarding at the end but is usually not much fun along the way for either party. Compromise is very tempting and works occasionally. In the long run however, compromise "compromises" the mindset for growth critical to a program's progress. The lure of compromise also tests the head coach's mettle for sustaining a vision for the program and for enduring outside pressures. Having assistants at the lower levels who understand the program's mentality for molding these learners into the "education type" and out of the "run and sit" type of teammate is desirable.

What coaches must accomplish is gaining the players' respect. Popularity is a distant second. Head coaches should have some absolute, non-negotiable standards, lines so to speak that cannot be crossed. However, a little unpredictability is also healthy to a player-coach relationship. A coach's primary responsibility is to be someone players can count on to make the right call for the progress of both the individual player and the team. At times, those decisions will be difficult. Making those decisions regarding both the player and the team's welfare ultimately shape the direction of the program and go well beyond a won-loss record. With every difficult decision, coaches make every attempt to think team first. There will be successes and failures along the way. Leaders must recognize which type of learner they are dealing with that provides the best course to achieve the ultimate goal of team chemistry. Allowing the whole to be greater than the sum of the parts educates every player's mindset for growth in a maximum number of ways.

 REFLECTION

TOM ANSTETT

In the season of 1981-82, on the Saturday evening before the start of the state tournament, the school sponsored a turnabout dance at our school. Girl asks boy. A nice event, but I worried about dances, and head coaches know the reasons. We played our first game the following Tuesday. Come Monday, the dean of students informed me that one of my starters, a good strong forward, was found to have open liquor in his car on school premises the night of the dance. Although we had no athletic code per se in that year, from the start of the season I had made my position clear to the team about drinking, smoking, and drugs. Depending on the facts, any incident carried some degree of suspension, maybe even expulsion from the team. I met with my coaches, then the team, and told the player in question he was not playing that entire first week in the regional tournament. We had enjoyed a 20-win season and were a favorite to win the regional and advance. The players felt betrayed and were more upset at the player than at me, which substantiated the right collective mentality we had nurtured in the program year after year: team first. The rest of the team bonded and battled in the tournament. On the other hand, my decision was met with some angst from the student body. Students carried banners into the game, big enough for the head coach to see with the suspended player's name. They chanted, "Put in ---!!" From my seat, a bit warmer than usual, there was no chance he was playing. As it turned out, we advanced to the title game, but lost. I had no regrets, and as it turned out, that one player and I are good friends today. Moreover, that incident reinforced the growth we expected in our program, serving as an example of a non-negotiable to all of our returning players. I went so far as to explain my decision to my English classes which cooled some of the angst and fostered more trust from everyone in that present time and in the future.

In today's culture, schools try to cover their behinds with as much paperwork as the local lumber yard will allow. Coaches need more in writing where parents and players sign oaths called a "Code of Conduct" or a similar title. Consequently, there is more pressure on coaches to educate their players about all the distractions which can damage whatever positive mentality the coaches have tried to instill in the program. So, a conundrum follows when situations like the above occur. Do coaches stick to their guns and show players that the program's ethics are more important than any one player, or do they cower to administrators, most of whom rarely attend games and really do not care if the team wins or loses, as long as the number of participants is healthy for the school report card and there are no problems? I refer to two epic quotations from literature to fortify my answer: "To thine own self be true." (Shakespeare) and "I took the road less traveled by and that has made all the difference" (Robert Frost).

MOVE OVER, ALBERT EINSTEIN...

With all due respect, we present a new formula pertaining to athletics:

E2 + M = P2
(EXCELLENT EXECUTION + MASTERY = POSSIBLE PERFECTION)

EXCELLENCE=

Learning and applying everything you can
about what you are doing.

EXECUTION=

The achievement of the required detail
and technique under pressure

MASTERY=

Comprehensive knowledge or skill
in a subject or accomplishment.

PERFECTION=

The condition, action, state, or quality of being free
or as free as possible from all flaws or defects

In our own pursuit of the highest standard of achievement for our programs, coaches sometimes get lost in the pursuit of perfection. Playing the perfect game or having the perfect season becomes a noble, but unattainable driving force, one which leads us to never be completely satisfied no matter what the outcome. For the underdog, victory is sheer jubilation. For the favorite, victory is often relief. Losing is always misery.

Coach Rollie Massimino's Villanova team came about as close to playing the perfect game as any college team ever had in its victory in the 1985 national championship game against Georgetown. Coach Bob Williams's Schaumburg

High School team's victory against Thornwood High School in the 2001 Illinois 2A state championship game was another remarkable example. There is no doubt that in order to accomplish what those two teams did took performances of near perfection. Those two coaches and their players were so attentive to the details of excellence in execution and mastery that when the opportunity for the ultimate prize presented itself, they were ready for the challenge and the "perfect" game. At any level of basketball, winning the title is a pinnacle; however, there is much more that tells the story of a season, playing career, or coaching career. Some coaches chase perfection, but we suggest the pursuit of excellence as a team supported by a mastery of the game for individual players as the motivation that drives the team and players. For example, we consider a turnover number of 12 or fewer as a reasonable goal for most games. 12 turnovers are hardly perfection, but excellence of team performance and mastery of individual ballhandling and passing skill may certainly have been achieved. Thus, a level for excellence for any one team is a variable determined by the level of talent and the empowering, collective mentality of both coaches and players.

 REFLECTION

TOM McCORMACK

Sometimes in order to pursue excellence and mastery of the game, a coach has to be willing to "prune the tree." Players sometimes fall into a state of what we called "good enough is good enough." This is a state of mind that inhibits the growth potential of any team.

There were a couple of seasons when my teams fell into this stagnation just after the Christmas tournament. Both teams were winning games but did not have the type of leadership where the best players were the hardest workers. Practice resembled a trip to the dentist to have a tooth drilled-without the Novocain. Our first seven in the playing rotation had gone from a growing and learning team to a sit and run, stagnant group.

I do not recommend this next step without trying several, less drastic tactics first. After two weeks of going through the motions at practice, it was either act now or risk underachievement for the rest of the season. When we came to the scrimmages at the end of practice, the second unit had been beating our first group consistently both weeks. We had played just well enough to win our last game. Actually, we only scored just enough. Our players were playing just good enough with effort and execution.

On the Wednesday before our Friday game, the first group was still being outworked. So, I announced that tomorrow Thursday, usually a lighter preparation day, was instead going to be an all-out scrimmage between the first seven and the second team. The winners would play in the varsity game and the losers would play in the J-V game Saturday morning. We were playing a strong opponent on Friday. The outcome meant just not starting the game or not playing in the first quarter. It meant the winners of the scrimmage were in the playing rotation the entire game; the losers would not play one minute.

At Thursday's practice, the scrimmage was 25 points, so what could go wrong? The first group surely had enough time to gear it up so they couldn't lose on a fluke, right? Wrong. Exactly as they had for the last two weeks, the second team outhustled and outplayed the first team and won the scrimmage. Not the dilemma any coach wants to experience, but the entitlement needed to be pruned, even if it cost us a game. I had drawn a line in the sand, and the first unit had crossed it. When this situation happens, there are three options. Ignore it like it never happened; modify the action with a stiff warning; or stay true to your word. The first two options are akin to Animal House and Double Secret Probation-and just as useless. Flexibility is a great trait for a head coach, but this was a Pat Riley "Plant your feet" moment for the team, me, and the coaching staff. There were no options. The second unit played the entire game on Friday.

At the following Monday's practice, I kept the squad in their reversed roles and told our new second team that they had to dominate every scrimmage that week to play next Friday. They dominated the scrimmages and drill work was a war. They won back their first team roles. We had very few intensity problems the rest of the year.

Fortunately, I had an athletic director who had my back with this action. I suggest that if you have to take action that is fairly drastic like this one was, you have to know your administration and who your allies are. Keep them in the loop, ahead of time if possible. In some cases-and this case I thought was one-the action must be taken regardless of the fallout, administrative support or not. There was some fallout, mostly on the part of our fans and a few parents, but as the NBA legendary coach Hubie Brown once said, "Dogs bark, but the caravan moves on."

After taking some time to reflect on the entire situation, I thought that while the action was needed, I should have handled several things better with the players, coaches, and the A.D. I had asked a lot of that group and our great fans. I asked them to trust me.

I told our assistant coaches we needed to find a better way next time. They should not allow me to repeat that decision. Remember the line in Hoosiers when Coach Dale gets thrown out of the game and tells Shooter, "I did it again"? Two years later in the same situation and against an even better opponent, I issued the same challenge. You guessed it. The second team beat the first team again, only this time my son Matt, our best screener, hustler, and charge taker, was one of the first seven. He sat on the bench on that Friday like everyone else in the first group.

Making the tough call was necessary, a responsibility a head coach has to face head on. Head coaches sometimes have to risk losing the job for the right reasons to survive in the long run and keep both job and integrity. One is quite meaningless without the other.

By the way, our second unit won both those varsity games. Naturally, we were very proud of them and just as proud of the way both units responded the rest of the season. We became a better practice team and kept improving our collective mindset for excellence the rest of the season. Both groups of players made it to the Elite Eight in the state tournament. E2 + M = P2...the hard way.

SOME "WHAT IFs...?"
FOR MENTALITY, THE MINDSET FOR GROWTH

Coaches, what if...

...the team is playing selfishly?

This issue might center on one or two players. If so, sit them down and show them the evidence-perhaps with one player at a time. If no positive response occurs at subsequent practices, remove the player(s) from the playing rotation after the weekend so practice can determine the new unit(s). See if the player(s) in question respond well with the second unit and observe if more unselfish team play happens with the new lineup.

If unselfishness dominates your team in general, consider this. Put five players on the floor in position to run your half-court offense. Give each player his or her own basketball and watch the chaos that ensues when you say, "Now run our offense." It's similar to watching The Three Stooges. In fact, you only need two basketballs to accomplish the same thing. Watch the arguing, the frustration, and the confusion unfold. See what players possess the dexterity to catch two or three balls simultaneously. If the team does not respond to your first effort, we recommend drills like passing for points (explained in the Guts chapter) where the only path to victory is sharing the ball. Failing that, a little run and sit may be in order.

...the team has cliques?

Cliques can destroy a team's mentality, even if a strong mindset already exists. Cliques mean leaderless stereotypes and exclusiveness. They can hinder any true teamwork. From a coaching standpoint, it is important to divide and conquer. Mix up teams at practice. Make each member of the clique a captain of a drill group; then do the opposite. Another idea is to install a buddy system where the coach pairs up two teammates who aren't necessarily compatible. This system helps to bring players of diverse backgrounds together for a common purpose.

...the team is underachieving to its talent?

This span of a season can cause dismay and utter frustration for a coach who approached the season thinking big. Lots of communication is needed and much of that communication is through game film. Is the team executing the fundamentals well? Sometimes, going back to Basic Basketball 101 will alleviate simple errors or carelessness that have led to bizarre and unacceptable losses to teams of less talent. This retraining will consist of observing, explaining, drilling, and using visual, auditory, and kinetic learning styles. These players are often willing learners. Their talent lies more in the physical tools, but the mental edge has to be explored and improved. Coaches have to examine the players' physical conditioning to further develop their physical and mental toughness. Whatever the case, coaches cannot let up on them, thinking that it is only a matter of time before their talent shows up. Above all, coaches should not lower expectations, but coaches also need to examine their own techniques and philosophy to see if changes are needed. Many times, perseverance is the only thing separating success from failure.

...the team is a poor practice team?

The first step is to examine the reasons for poor practices. Some reasons might be boredom, low morale, softness, a losing streak, a winning streak, or selfishness. There are others. In one scenario players see practices as drudgery, the last thing coaches want to detect. So, the more competition within drills and scrimmages, the better. Coaches should try to be unpredictable in the types of drills, the lengths of them, and the forms of scrimmages. Separating the drills with brief scrimmages might be helpful; that pattern means having a couple of drills, then having players scrimmage for five minutes, but with the players choosing sides and with one player coaching his or her team. Keeping a precise and upbeat tempo is important for any practice with a team that is apathetic about the work. Filming practice followed by debriefing with the team is in order. Perhaps have a knowledgeable, retired coach observe the team at practice and report on his/her findings. Former NBA guard Allen Iverson made the comment, "Practice; it's just practice." How many championships did his teams win? Try zero. Compare him to Michael Jordan who was the best practice player on his Chicago Bulls' teams and their six NBA championships. Share that comparison with teams that practice to just finish it, instead of using the practice hours to improve in skills and in teamwork in order to win.

A second scenario is the inability of the second team to provide tough, consistent competition for the first team. That undesirable often confronts many grade school and high school coaches. Try as they might, the second team players fall short and provide the starters with a false sense of security. Coaches have to be imaginative in their drills and often distort the game by giving advantages to the second team in scrimmages and drills. Over the course of a season, coaches might detect some good improvements in the second team's individual abilities with continuous motivation and praise of the second unit at every opportunity.

In all cases, coaches have to determine the source of the problem. Determining the source will lead to the best path for solving the issue.

...the parents of the best player interfere with your approach to the team's growth?

In this situation the player is caught in the middle. Does he/she listen more to mixed messages from the parent or from the coach? The head coach has to rely on evaluations of the player at practice; those observations are the hard evidence for the amount of playing time and the role for the player in question. This potentially chaotic situation can divide a team. Coaches might find they pay an undue amount of attention to the player instead of to the team's progress, and the rest of the team will be quick to detect that overt attention. It is similar to the one reluctant, interfering student in one class; that classroom teacher finds much of his/her waking thoughts focus on one student instead of the grand scheme. Very distracting and counterproductive. One meeting with the parents can be helpful with the player in question in attendance and an assistant coach. No player present equals no meeting. The player must be in attendance to hear the discussion, hear the observations from the coach about the player's work habits at practices, and know the continued expectations from the coach. One note about the meeting: let the parent speak first. The coach should take notes for any rebuttal; the documentation can come in handy later, if the parents leave the meeting unsatisfied and try to go beyond the coach to an administrator for satisfaction. However, the main emphasis is the player. Is the player clear about future direction and personal improvement that benefit the team? Is the player's mindset for growth on an upward trajectory? A follow-up conference with that player is helpful because at that meeting, the player can talk more freely without the parent. Divide and conquer.

...the best players are juniors or sophomores, causing resentment from the seniors?

Any senior who makes the team has to have a definite role with some playing time. Seniors who see no action are possible time bombs for team unity. Why do coaches keep seniors who will not play? Any senior who accepts that role possesses true character, but it is a long season and maintaining that unselfishness can bolster a team if it is sustained. Thus, coaches need to see the big picture when evaluating juniors, those seniors-to-be.

Another aspect to this question is the decision to raise a freshman or sophomore to the varsity. That action can cause plenty of resentment. Has that player been with the team all summer? If so, tension eases since everyone knows the skills of the young player in question and realizes the ways that player can help the team win. The player should be physically mature enough to handle the physical nature of varsity competition or why bother? If the physical talent is present, is the prospect emotionally tough enough to handle the bigger limelight? A key decision. However, the bottom line for any lifting of a freshman or a sophomore to the varsity is skill level, especially passing. Young players have a tendency to commit turnovers. Does that player have the skills to compete and contribute? Does that player fill a need for the team's completion? Those considerations are all parts of preparation.

...players on your team are doing off-season workouts for fall or spring sports during your season?

This unfortunate occurrence should not happen. In the majority of cases, the fault lies not with the athlete, but with selfish coaches who influence, inflate egos, even intimidate their star players to attend early morning workouts in order to be a "star(ter)" in their next season: the quarterback, the best hitter, the gifted running back, etc. Head basketball coaches need to meet with that particular head coach for an upfront discussion with the outcome that favors the in-season sport. Unlike parents who might immediately go over the head of a classroom teacher when their child is unhappy or receives an unsatisfactory grade, the basketball coach, in this case, should take the disagreement one step at a time. An initial meeting with the other coach is in order; if there is no agreement, seeing the athletic director to voice the concern is a next step. Hopefully, the trail ends there.

...programs in the summer conflict with basketball?

Before conflicts happen, head coaches should meet to discuss and agree on sharing multi-athletes throughout the summer. Once they agree on conditions, each coach must follow through. One suggestion here from a basketball standpoint is for those head coaches to ask for a 50-50 split from their athletes in question. For example, if John/Jane Doe has a conflict one night between choosing to attend a basketball league game or a football 7 on 7, John/Jane can choose where to go. However, the next time there is a similar conflict, that player must attend the sport missed the previous time. In any event, good communication among head coaches sends a positive message to the athletes that everyone is working together, thus creating more trust and support among the sports. That healthy environment makes for a better school.

...your player wants to skip either practices or games (or both) over a weekend to make a college recruiting visit?

A tough one. No head coach wants to be a distraction to a player's potential college choice, but distractions run both ways. An important contributor to a basketball team who decides to leave for the weekend for a football visit and miss practices or important games can create distrust and animosity with the rest of the team. On the other hand, that decision might be small potatoes to the team. Ultimately, it depends on the manner that coach presents his/her position to the player and to the team. Hopefully, this type of issue has been discussed in pre-season meetings and the team's expectations. The former coach of the Chicago Bulls, Tom Thibodeau, responded to injuries or distractions with the statement, "Next man up." Parallel to that position, if an important player goes on the trip, it is an opportunity for the sub or the second team player to take advantage and play well. The big picture probably takes precedence. Looking at the bright side can be beneficial for everyone, even though any coach wants the whole team ready for battle at every game.

...a talented and promising athlete is having a hard time fitting into the program?

It might be the type of player with the potential to take the team to a higher level or a kid who might just fit a role on a team. Some of the reasons might be a tough home life, learning disabilities, undue outside influences, a move from a different area, economic hardship, helicopter parents, just plain spoiled, etc. In any case, dealing with this type of player can disrupt team chemistry. Sometimes the player is more in need of the team than the team is in need of the player. Remember in the movie Hoosiers when coach Dale tells Jimmy Chitwood, after rebounding a few shots for him, "I don't care if you play or not." Every young person wants to be a part of something. The first step is to make that player feel welcome so a level of trust can begin to develop. Enlisting the aid of the team's leaders and the coaching staff is very helpful. A buddy system with a reliable player, a school counselor, and maybe a key classroom teacher are all also helpful resources.

Even though coaches can take on the role of a pseudo-psychologist in dealing with these types of players, oftentimes the coach taking this player onto the team might be the player's only chance for mature development. The player might even have star potential he/she doesn't realize. This player needs boundaries, just like the rest of the team, not limits. Boundaries, similar to role definitions, do not limit, but actually help focus and center the struggling player past previous limitations. Boundaries also help the rest of the team buy in if the coach has to show some flexibility with that player. One size does not fit all. You will win some and you will lose some, but the effort to help must be honest and steady. After all, why do we coach?

Many people sitting in the stands think your job is simple and is nothing but Xs and Os and who plays. Little do they know of all the plates you have to keep spinning. A wise athletic director had the best advice, "Think first, and do what you know in your heart is the right thing."

...a thunderbolt strikes?

What if the team loses its best or a key player for a portion of the season, or worse, for the entire season? In his book *The Winner Within*, Pat Riley calls these situations "thunderbolts."

Thunderbolts will hit at some point, whether it occurs in a marriage, a team, or a corporation. Some are the types that can be predicted based on an unseen or anticipated buildup before the dark cloud on the horizon becomes the storm on top of the particular group or organization. For example, a player becomes ineligible at the semester for the rest of the season when the weekly grade check reports had indicated a need for some intervention. With their eyes and ears open to the whole program and their delegated responsibilities, assistant coaches are a great asset in avoiding these situations.

Usually, thunderbolts strike suddenly, such as the season ending injury, a transfer to another school, or a key player quitting just before the season starts to concentrate on another sport. Consider what Coach Riley says about dealing with these crises, "Giving yourself permission to lose guarantees a loss. If you don't steel yourself to people's sympathy, you cheat yourself and your dream. Shoulda, coulda, and woulda won't get it done. In attacking adversity, only a positive attitude, alertness, and re-grouping to basics can launch a comeback...Coming back from a thunderbolt has little to do with a grand strategy and a great deal to do with strength of heart and the conviction to follow a basic plan."

When a thunderbolt hits, if excellence and mastery have been established as the program's pillars and the mindset for growth, then the next move may not be easy to do, but it will be clear to see. We as coaches are a resilient group by the nature of our chosen profession.

The following ingredients exhibit courage for a basketball player. Each action requires unselfishness. Each action promotes team spirit. Each action inspires growth for the player's mindset. Each action contributes to winning. Each action contributes to the development of the person, as well as the player.

- Taking the charge

- Setting as many good screens as possible

- Cutting hard

- Rebounding in a crowd

- Diving "Superman" style for loose balls

- Boxing out after every shot

- Positive body language after both defeats and victories

- Staying in a defensive stance every possession

- Taking criticism in the right way

- Looking at the coach when being criticized

- Running extra or lifting extra after workouts

- Exceeding, not just meeting, goals

- Taking the big shot…after missing one

- Denying the ball to an opponent

- Taking the opponent's star player out of the game with defense

- Making pressure free throws

- Taking weight training seriously—the more time in the weight room, the tougher players become

- Being invaluable without being most valuable

- Taking no prisoners inside the lines in practices and games but being a human being outside those lines

A FEW KEY COMPONENTS FOR IMPROVING A TEAM'S MENTALITY

1. VISUALIZATION

Bob Knight, former head coach at Indiana University, stated at a clinic, "Mental is to physical as four is to one." If that axiom is true, why don't coaches in every sport spend more time on the mental preparation necessary for top performances? Teaching basketball players methods for visualization is essential for improved practice habits that transfer to game production, not infrequent exceptions. Players and coaches should make the time for brief, effective minutes to visualize their performances. These mental preps can be done at home, before practices and games, on bus rides, or during leisure time. Kinesthetic, auditory, and visual sensations are all valid. This technique complements, does not substitute for, the work that needs to be done.

The technique is simple. The subconscious does not know the difference between the real and the imagined. Players sit in a comfortable spot, close their eyes, and visualize doing a certain skill or game situation with good achievement. The memory might be an action they are not doing well at the time. The visualizing pictures an upcoming game complete with noise, fouls, uniforms, sweat, etc. The idea is to make each visualization as real and as specific as possible. If done daily, improvement and a more positive self-image will follow. None of that process happens overnight. Like any attempt to instill or break a habit, three weeks of daily dedication to the task is a typical length of time to begin to see results.

 REFLECTION

TOM ANSTETT

Matt played point guard for me at York High School in Elmhurst, Illinois, from 1991-93. He was one of those players who disliked practices but rose to amazing heights in games. He wasn't much from a physical standpoint, standing about 6' and weighing 150. However, he had the guts and the internal machine of a true competitor, unafraid of the big moments. One of his most salient traits was his mental preparation come Thursday and game days. A few hours before every game, mainly after school, there he was in the gym, alone with a ball, dribbling up and down, visualizing potential moves against the opponent that night. He epitomized vivid imagination as a powerful tool for his game's success. It was no wonder that his terrific game performances followed. Moreover, I provided as part of the pre-game prep in the locker room some minutes for quiet visualization for the entire team, coaches included.

2. READING ABOUT THE GAME

Both coaches and players should read about the game they love. So often, today's players have little knowledge of the game's great players or history. Reading inspires players for living a more productive life, overcoming obstacles, and developing good practice habits. Every summer we assigned at least one basketball-related book for everyone in the program. The goal was for the players to have read the book by the time summer camps were over. We then had a discussion of the book in a group setting.

Here are some possibilities. Few of these books contain much basketball strategy or Xs and Os. These authors offer a positive, relentless mentality for improved competitiveness.

My Losing Season, Pat Conroy

Stop Whining; Start Winning: For Teachers and Coaches, Tom Anstett

Jordan Rules, Sam Smith

Attitude and *Team Building: From the Bench to the Boardroom*, Pat Sullivan

The Last Pass: Cousy, Russell, the Celtics, and What Matters in the End, Gary Pomerantz

Sacred Hoops, Phil Jackson

Pistol, The Life of Pete Maravich, Mark Kreigel

The Miracle of St. Anthony's, Adrian Wojnarowski

A Season on the Brink and The Last Amateurs, John Feinstein

The Fab Five, Mitch Albom

Heaven is a Playground, Rick Telander

Drive-The Story of My Life, Larry Bird

Life on the Run and Values of the Game, Bill Bradley

Russell Rules and *Go Up for Glory*, Bill Russell

Leading From the Heart, Mike Kryzewzski

Larry Bird/Magic Johnson—When the Game Was Ours, Jackie McMullen

The Breaks of the Game, David Halberstam

The Smart Take from the Strong, Pete Carril

Basketball FundaMENTALs, Jay Mikes

Creative Coaching, Jerry Lynch

A Passion to Lead, Jim Calhoun

The Winner Within, Pat Riley

Basketball on Paper, Dean Oliver

Runnin' the Show, Dick Devenzio

Play Their Hearts Out, George Dohrmann

On Becoming a Leader, Warren Bennis

Coaches of Chicago, Paul Pryma

Toughness, Jay Bilas

Wooden on Leadership, John Wooden

Winning Every Day: The Game Plan for Success and *Wins, Losses, and Lessons*, Lou Holtz

Why The Best Are The Best, Kevin Eastman

[The list is endless and we encourage your communicating other titles to the authors and to your peers.]

3. WHY DO YOU COACH?

In each summer or pre-season, take the time to list your basketball tenets. These tenets are the principles for which you coach. They identify what you stand for as a coach and what you demand from your players. They fortify your own mentality and can be the rocks of the program. Some examples:

- Our team's point guard is my extension on the floor. He must know what I am thinking and/or want at certain moments.

- Our team must be in top condition.

- Fundamentals represent the backbone in our program, so we must teach them well.

- Strive for excellence, not perfection.

- I will look at both kids and colleagues with my eyes, my brain, and my heart. One, maybe two of those assets will deliver what I need.

4. TAKE A "TEACHER-FIRST" MENTALITY

High school programs today are often in conflict with the AAU mentality which says, "Shop around until you find one you like and get what you want." The typical high school program says, or at least used to say, "These types of players are what we have; here is how we are going to make it work, and we are going to hang in there together until we do or at least give it our best shot." However, it is unfair to categorize all AAU programs and coaches the same; some are excellent and some, not so much.

AAU programs do have the advantage of working with kids who are only basketball players and hungry to improve their individual games. High school coaches are fortunate if they have a few of these types of players, and they sometimes have to convince and depend on multiple-sport athletes to join the program, often at the varsity level.

Certain advantages the high school coach has are the daily interaction and contact in and out of season, more practice time, a better facility, and a teacher's mentality. That last approach leads to better quality, communication, and organization in the structure of the individual team and the whole program. Coaches seize opportunities to meet with their players individually throughout the season and school year, opportunities that build good relationships with every person on the team for the most part. High school coaches' classroom experiences and rigor translate to better application of the details that support a quality program. A majority of high school coaches have that teaching background. Many of the AAU coaches do not. Furthermore, coaches are paid as teachers first; coaching stipends are secondary. We hope that fact alone motivates coaches to be quality teachers, no matter the time of day. We feel head coaches should strive to be the best classroom teachers in their schools.

For both high school and AAU players, being a starter is a primary goal with playing time a close second. If either goal is unachieved, players might transfer or become a team distraction. We rarely referred to any of our players as starters, either to themselves, the newspaper, or other public forum. We preferred to say, "These five players are going to be in at the beginning of the game, but if you are really asking me who are best five are, let's see who finishes." We tried to sell that belief to our players that the overarching goals should be to finish the close games and to stick with the program through both the good and the tough times. Those lessons by themselves give programs immense credibility and promote the ideal of total player-person development and empowerment. Those invaluable lessons filter through the entire school.

All of the above stem from the importance of coaches' taking a teacher-first mentality. That distinct approach requires coaches to provide goals, create clear and insightful plans, and evaluate progress-just like a classroom. With that consistent approach, the high school coach can significantly influence a player's direction in life, sometimes the most meaningful and lasting influence. Shopping around has its place, but a place below working through the choices and commitments everyone in a basketball program makes on and off the court.

5. COMFORT VS. DISCOMFORT— PLAYER "MUST-KNOWS" = COACHES "MUST TEACH"

Players must learn how to be comfortable when being uncomfortable. How? They push themselves to a greater height of mental motivation in the moment. For example, when players are getting back on defense, they might think that the upcoming stop is the most vital in the entire game. On offense they simplify their movements and see the game in slow motion. During sprints or other conditioning, they evaluate themselves by the stopwatch that never lies.

Players must know the teaching of the coach thoroughly. Coaches should implement that instruction through quick, planned tempos at practices. A former Creighton University coach once stated, "Mental quickness is more important than physical quickness."

Players must accept the mentality that shortcuts do not exist in the program. Nothing worthwhile is accomplished without hard work, careful planning, dreaming big, and efficient workouts.

Players must ingrain the "disposition to dominate on defense" (Knight) every time they step onto the court. Pain is part of that success.

Players must develop a belief in the end-of-the-game teaching and execution.

6. LEADERSHIP DEVELOPMENT

Although never within a certain time frame, leadership can emerge first in the off-season. Why? Much off-season participation is voluntary; any player aspiring to be a leader shows up regularly. Leadership is difficult; if it was easy, everyone would have a Ph.D. Who are the leaders on your team? Examine why they are leaders. What responsibilities do you give them? Keep in mind what Michael Jordan said in the recent documentary *The Last Dance*, "I never asked anybody to do anything I didn't do. Never."

On the other hand, leadership does not have to evolve around one or two players. Ever examine the condition of your locker room after players leave for home after practices? How about the visiting locker room after games? See rolls of tape, litter, towels, or garbage on the floor? We insisted on clean locker rooms. If players ignored that guideline or disrespected our managers, they paid a price called "Attitude Adjustment." Respect is a two-way street and players need to understand the importance to give it first. As Coach McCormack puts it, "It is easier to replace a player than a good manager."

Then, there is the eloquent verse
by Lao-Tzu, Chinese philosopher:

In the leader's desire to be at the front of people,
He must in his person be behind them.
In his desire to be above the principles,
he must in his speech be below them.
Sincere words are not showy,
Showy words are not sincere.
Those who know do not say;
Those who say do not know.

7. PATIENCE

The renowned basketball coach William Shakespeare said, "He that will have cake out of the wheat must tarry the grinding" (quoted in The Plays of William Shakespeare, Isaac Reed, 737). He implies the use of patience, an undercurrent throughout this book and a trait never to be confused with complacency. Remember earlier when we said that success occurs when preparation and opportunity meet? Patience is meaningless if the physical and mental preparation has not been laid as a foundation first. Most coaches, us included, have had to work their way up with plenty of patience and resilience. Handling rejection is an obstacle that has ended many coaching and playing careers. One of the greatest lessons to be learned from patience is to control what we can control and avoid overanalyzing what we cannot control. Our levels of work, study, and preparation are controllable factors. Surely, stepping back from time to time to assess the direction we are taking to a goal is healthy for progress, but when rejections or setbacks occur, they are opportunities to learn and grow, not give up or completely change a planned direction. This outlook applies to players looking for a role on the team, coaches evaluating an individual game or season, or both players and coaches determining the path of their playing or coaching careers. If the right amount of preparation occurs, the right amount of patience leads to improvement with a clearer thought process. Players and coaches need the patience to wait for opportunity to present itself and the resilience to bounce back from rejection. Resilience is a form of patience.

Arguably, patience remains one of the toughest virtues to possess and model, especially in this era of the desire to attain results "today by yesterday." Coaches retain a terrific platform to model patience with young people, thereby teaching a wonderful lesson that anything worthwhile takes time to create and develop. As mentioned earlier, one definition of excellence is "learning everything you can about what you are doing." That definition underscores the importance of learning patience and with that patience comes the resilience to finish what one has begun. In this last letter of "P-R-O-G-R-A-M," patience just might be a last word to remember for coaches who want to build and sustain a quality basketball program. Being a part of a great program as a player or a coach does not guarantee constant success, but if coaches patiently teach the details of the game well while demanding accountability from their players, there will be more celebrations of progress rather than long faces of defeat. More poise follows.

Henry David Thoreau, the 19th century Transcendentalist, said it well in his famous analogy in his journal *Walden*: "Everyone has heard the story which has gone the rounds of New England, of a strong and beautiful bug which came out of a dry leaf of an old table of apple-tree wood, which had stood in a farmer's kitchen for sixty years, first in Connecticut, and afterward in Massachusetts-from an egg deposited in the living tree many years earlier still, as appeared by counting the annual layers beyond it; which was heard gnawing out for several weeks, hatched perchance by the heat of an urn. Who does not feel his faith in a resurrection and immortality strengthened by hearing of this? Who knows what beautiful and winged life, whose egg has been buried for ages under many concentric layers of woodenness in the dead dry life of society, deposited at first in the alburnum of the green and living tree, which has been gradually converted into the semblance of its well-seasoned tomb-heard perchance gnawing out now for years by the astonished family of man, as they sat round the festive board-may unexpectedly come forth from amidst society's most trivial and handselled furniture, to enjoy its perfect summer at last!"

Translation: Talent and successful goal attainment take time to reveal themselves, but when they do, enjoy the fruits of the labor. Exactly the reason for coaches to be patient with everyone in the program, down to the last player on the freshman "B" team.

8. A PROGRESSIVE MINDSET FOR GROWTH FOR ONE SEASON

We liked to tell players the non-conference teams we played were tough; conference play was tougher; and the playoffs were the toughest. Each sequence required enhanced toughness and both individual and team improvement.

9. TOUGH MENTALITY LEARNED ON THE COURT
CAN LAST A LIFETIME

ATTITUDE. In a plethora of ways, Bill Schaefer taught and modeled excellence to both of us as young coaches. He and his wife Linda possessed tough mentality and steady friendship. They were a great team: Linda the quiet, thoughtful deliberate to Bill's energetic, humorous persona. They raised four fine children, including Steven who died in a fire at Southern Illinois University during his college years while attempting to save others from a burning building.

In the spring of 1995, Linda was working out at a YMCA and training for a hike into the Grand Canyon with her girlfriends. Driving home, she experienced a sudden brain seizure. She hit other vehicles and was transported to the hospital. After tests, doctors discovered that she had a cancerous, inoperable brain tumor. The news jolted everyone who knew the family. In similar situations, some families might sit back and wait for the inevitable. Not Bill. He did not sit back. With his immense curiosity for the unknown, Bill researched potential treatments that were not FDA-approved. He argued with Linda's doctors, bringing new ideas and names with the hopes of the doctors' trying these ideas. Bill did not settle for the same old thing. His tireless intensity brought hope to Linda who gave similar energy to Bill.

That is exactly how a good program works. Its members supply energy, and the energy is returned. As the late Steve Jobs stated in his 2004 commencement address at Stanford University, "Don't settle."

BALANCE. As a boy, Ulysses S. Grant, the 18th President of the United States, was labeled "Useless." His peers at West Point continued that name. Society often is too quick to underestimate young people who are just scratching the surface of their talents in their teens, twenties, and thirties. Such was the case with Grant. As it turned out, "useless" he was not. Both the Mexican-American War and the Civil War showcased the talents he possessed for leadership and mental poise. Soldiers admired and followed his penchant for staying calm under pressure. As we know, Grant became the outstanding leader Abraham Lincoln needed to win the Civil War and begin to heal the country. Becoming president added to Grant's contributions to America. Grant modeled neither haughtiness nor a prima donna stature. His strong, steady mentality was an example for imitation, a trait necessary for any athletic success, work-related issues, and healthy relationships. What a point guard he would have made: instinctive and correct responses to situations, a faith in victory, a toughness to apply to a decision, and a way to transmit that toughness to the team under his command. The more coaches put pressure on their charges in practices, the more those coaches witness the growth of poise of his team members. Bill Schaefer had a prime definition for poise. "Do the job the way you learned the job, no matter the pressure or situation." President Grant lived that same way. If high school basketball players learn and apply better poise by the time they graduate, that is a gift that lasts. Useful will they be.

COMMUNICATION. Forrest Gump stated, "Stupid is as stupid does." A huge difference exists between stupidity and ignorance. An ignorant person does not know the methods desired by the teacher or the coach; that person can be educated and taught what to do with the hope he or she applies the instruction well. A stupid person or player knows what to do but makes the same mistakes in that area of instruction over and over. Stupid players lose; they cannot be coached; they know what to do but refuse to listen or do the correct way. We are willing to coach the ignorant any day. (If that player is quick, smart, and 6'8"—all the better!) With good instruction and communication, coaches build the right mentality within the ignorant. Their progress can be astounding. Moreover, everyone starts ignorant which is one reason we treasure good teachers and coaches.

DETERMINATION. In planning and preparing to fulfill his dream, a businessman and serious pilot overviewed prospective areas from his cockpit for building his stores. That pilot was none other than Sam Walton, founder of Walmart. The history of Walmart, an American discount department store chain, began in 1950 when he purchased a store from Luther E. Harrison in Bentonville, Arkansas, and opened Walton's 5 & 10. At that moment, a marketing and business giant was born. Sam Walton believed running a successful business boils down to 10 simple rules. These rules have helped Walmart become the global leader it is today.

We connect each of Walton's rules to the coaching profession. These connections can build more strength in the necessary mentality for running a basketball program.

1. Commit to your business.

Walton: Believe in it more than anybody else. If you love your work, you'll be out there every day trying to do it the best you possibly can, and pretty soon everybody around will catch the passion from you like a fever.

Coach: You cannot fool players. They know if you are invested in your work and in them. Love the players. Find out what makes each tick. Follow through with them after they leave.

2. Share your profits with all your associates and treat them as partners.

Walton: In turn, they will treat you as a partner, and together you will all perform beyond your wildest expectations.

Coach: Make it a goal to invest in your assistants in as many ways as possible. Good assistants are your blood flow traveling to and through every player in the program.

Sam Walton

3. Motivate your partners.

Walton: Money and ownership alone aren't enough. Set high goals, encourage competition, and then keep score. Don't become too predictable.

Coach: Most coaches don't make much money, so that comparison falls well short. However, setting high, yet attainable expectations relevant to the talent, earns credibility. Change practice format once in a while. Keep players' curiosity high. Curiosity, whether in the classroom or in the athletic arena, is a paramount asset for increasing athletes' investment and improvement.

 REFLECTION

TOM ANSTETT

As an example, when I was coaching a sophomore team toward the end of my career, I assigned one boy per week to research a past player and report on that player to the entire team the next Thursday. Kareem, Dave Cowens, John Havlicek, Oscar Robertson were a few of the assignments. The players knew little of the cherished history of the game they played, so the players enjoyed this task. It was a fine way to relax a bit and learn about good models. Each player prepared a one-to-two-page report and made enough copies for every teammate. Those reports were part of each player's notebook.

4. Communicate everything you possibly can to your partners.

Walton: The more they know, the more they'll understand. The more they understand, the more they'll care. Once they care, there's no stopping them.

Coach: Knowledge is power. Communication, on and off the court, is a sign of caring.

5. Appreciate everything your associates do for the business.

Walton: Nothing else can quite substitute for a few well-chosen, well-timed, sincere words of praise. They're absolutely free and worth a fortune.

Coach: Do not wait for the end of a season to tell the players you love them, and you appreciate all the effort they are giving. This maxim holds for each individual as well as the entire team.

6. Celebrate your success.

Walton: Don't take yourself so seriously. Loosen up, and everybody around you will loosen up. Have fun. Show enthusiasm. All of this is more important, and more fun than you think, and it really fools competition.

Coach: On occasion and with good timing, surprise players with a get together, treats after a practice, the pool instead of practice, a competitive yet enjoyable shooting game at the end of a practice, 3 on 2 with players on offense vs. coaches on defense for ten minutes to finish practice.

7. Listen to everyone in your company.

Walton: Figure out ways to get them talking. To push responsibility down in your organization and to force good ideas to bubble up within it, you must listen to what your associates are trying to tell you.

Coach: Hold periodic meetings to get suggestions from players and to get a feel of morale, frustration, etc. Put tape over your mouth, take notes, and listen. Avoid commenting. You will often walk away from those gatherings with a couple good ideas. These meetings empower the players and humanize the coach.

8. Exceed your customers' expectations.

Walton: Give them what they want-and a little more. Make good on all your mistakes and don't make excuses. Apologize. Stand behind everything you do.

Coach: Make clear and keep your promises and/or expectations. If you cannot, explain why. Admit mistakes, especially when dealing with the press. Players need to know you have their backs especially in tough seasons.

Tell players it is okay, and even a sign of strength, to admit mistakes, express remorse, or admit ignorance about a question or topic. Coach Bo Ryan's recruiting philosophy was, "Under-promise and over-deliver," a refreshing change from some of the high-pressure, false promises athletes hear from some recruiters.

9. Control your expenses better than your competition.

Walton: This is where you can always find the competitive advantage. You can make a lot of different mistakes and still recover if you run an efficient operation. Or you can be brilliant and still go out of business if you're too inefficient.

Coach: Superior organization is essential for a successful, enduring program. How organized are you?

10. Swim upstream.

Walton: Go the other way. Ignore the conventional wisdom. If everybody else is doing it one way, there's a good chance you can find your niche by going in exactly the opposite direction.

(https://corporate.walmart.com/our-story/
history/10-rules-for-building-a-business)

Coach: First, being hard-nosed or stubborn about a certain system of play without fitting the talent level of a team leads to some form of disaster. Fit the style of play to the players' abilities. Second, be eager to try a different defense, if the players fit it. Always the man-to-man defense? Try an appropriate zone as part of a game plan. You might throw the opposing coach into a tizzy; after all, he or she prepared all week for a man-to-man defense. Overall, take opportunities to think beyond the plan, especially when preparing to play an opponent a second time.

 REFLECTION

TOM ANSTETT

Sophomore year at Quigley Seminary North, 1966-67, one of the roughest years of my existence. From a meandering mentality focused on 16-inch softball, I had "volunteered" to try basketball, with the entire goal to shut up my high school P.E. teacher and coach, Bill Schaefer, proving to him I was no good at hoop. He'd cut me; then I'd be rid of his hunting me down and pestering me to try basketball.

Little did I know. In more ways than one.

We started practices on October 1, early for teams nowadays, but that date was the state guideline. The first game was mid-November, so we had tons of time to hate each other. I thought I would make it through a few days, then be done. After he watched me play a skilled sport such as basketball, I was confident in only one aspect: Coach Schaefer would not desire to set his team back by years.

After two weeks, he told me, "Tom, you're going to be good." This statement made me question his sanity (something I often did for the next few years). He pronounced this statement after I had scored for the opponent in a scrimmage. Practices lasted close to three hours every day, except for Saturdays when each one seemed to last as long as Forrest Gump's cross country runs. After a couple more weeks, long after I discovered he was not cutting me, he kept me after one practice and told me I needed to get in better shape. He put me on the baseline and said he was timing me in "five each way," with down and back counting as one, so a total of ten sprints. Being momentarily stunned, I could not utter a wimp of protest. I did wonder why but prepared to run. "Get ready. Oh, and if you miss touching one baseline, you start over. Ready??" There was no discussion. No threats to call mommy. No desire to inform the superintendent tomorrow. I ran. He told me the time after the first set, which I cannot recall due to the brain damage I incurred during that season. Then he said, "Now you're going to run that series of sprints four more times, and you have to beat the previous time each one. If you miss one, you start over. Don't worry; we have tons of time! You have one minute to rest between sets." HE might have had tons of time, but I was thinking about my one-hour bus ride home and the three hours of homework that awaited.

As I pushed myself through the ordeal, I began to stomp on every baseline, imagining Schaefer's face below my size 15. The more I ran, the more I improved. Something inside of me, something I slowly became aware of, enveloped my psyche. That "something" was a competitiveness Coach Schaefer somehow knew I possessed, just as in my later coaching career, I saw and pushed in many of my players.

I don't know what made me complete the task without starting over, but when I limped into my house that night around 8:30, with those three hours of homework staring at me, I had overcome a challenge more mental than physical. My mother thought I looked like death. A correct assessment. My father asked me why I was dragging my ass. After I explained, he told me that the running was good for me. I was alone in an alien world. I had to decide to shrink or grow. I began to understand that I either make progress or make excuses. Putting a middle into those two choices leaves me behind.

Slowly, painfully, relentlessly, I was discovering the power of a strong mind. I stopped wondering about basketball and decided to make it part of my mentality and identity. Pushing past walls of pain became daily goals. The new mentality took no vacations. I became someone with a mindset for growth applicable to many areas of my life.

"The degree of players' mental toughness is in direct correlation to the quickness of their discouragement."

~Don McGee
Former Wheaton Central High School (Illinois) Head Coach

SUMMARY

PLANNING, ATTAINING, AND SUSTAINING
A GOOD BASKETBALL P-R-O-G-R-A-M

PREPARATION

Bo Ryan, former head coach at the University of Wisconsin, stated, "Plan your work and work your plan." How accurate is Coach Ryan's maxim? 100%, or as Coach Wooden said, "The will to win is insignificant unless the will to prepare to win is greater." Those two coaches' programs withstood the test of time. Preparation is like a car engine. It contains many parts. Each part contributes to a smooth ride. Each part requires time, knowledge, and commitment. Stalling on the highway to victory ruins the journey. Take the time to care for the engine.

RESILIENCE

"Do not judge me by my success. Judge me by how many times I fell down and got back up again." Nelson Mandela. Lasting programs are like rubber balls: tough, durable, and quick to bounce back. One victory only motivates a true program's teams to be hungrier for the next W. After all, it is easy to be mediocre; you don't have to do much.

OFF-SEASON

"In your dreams, you always win." Mike Krzyzewski. Dreaming big encourages quality players. Without efficient use of time and correct repetition, however, those dreams can become nightmares.

GUTS

"No guts. No glory. No legend. No story." (positivitysparkles.com) Can your team recover its attitude from poor play just through its relentless defense to an eventual victory? If not, victories are sparse, and any winning streaks are few and far between. The Hall of Fame coach Jack Ramsey said, "The opponent may have more talent, but our defense will be the great equalizer."

REBOUNDING

"No rebound, no ring." Pat Riley. A tough rebounder possesses the three intangibles present in The Wizard of Oz: a brain, a heart, and lots of courage.

ATTENTIVENESS

"Attention is the rarest and purest form of generosity." Simone Weil. Consistent and honest attentiveness reveals the notoriety of the coach and the unselfishness of the players. Eyes mirror souls.

MENTALITY

"If you see me fighting a bear, pray for the bear." Kobe Bryant. If you owned a fantastic racing car with plans to enter it into the Indianapolis 500, whom would you pick for the driver? The person with the toughest mindset, most proficient racing skill, and a mountain of poise.

We hope you have enjoyed the book and found at least a few things you can apply. As we explored the acronym P-R-O-G-R-A-M, we presented general, specific, technical, and practical information. Developing and evaluating your insights and curiosity were our main objectives. To that point, we hope this book has motivated you to explore each of the seven sections further to accelerate and reach your program's growth potential. Individually, each of the seven chapters of P-R-O-G-R-A-M could be a book unto itself. Who knows? Maybe we will still have some unfinished DETAILS to explore.

CONCLUSION...

Tom and Tom, coaches for the North-All Stars
at the IBCA game in Pontiac, 2017

THE HIGHER PURPOSE

There has to be a higher purpose to this game we all love than just putting the ball through the hoop. At times, we coaches are overcome by the temptations of building our own resumes and succumbing to the external pressures of outside expectations.

239

So, what is this higher purpose? Why is this fantastic game so much more than just a game?

None of us who has either coached or played at any level achieved that level or anything significant on our own. Who inspired and supported you? Have you thanked those significant others?

Giving back and paying it forward are two significant accomplishments of being part of a team. Our time is the most precious gift we can give. Besides being supporting alumni when the players move on, do they and/or your current team ever visit a nursing home, volunteer at a hospital, work a soup kitchen at the holidays, talk with and thank a veterans' group?

In the movie The Rookie, Dennis Quaid plays Jim Morris in the true story of a high school teacher and baseball coach in his late 30s. He gets the opportunity to play baseball again in the minor leagues and eventually makes it to the majors. One day as the younger players on the minor league team are standing around complaining about their current status, he enthusiastically jumps in the middle of the group and says, "Do you know what? Today we get to play baseball." There is a greater purpose and a simple one: joy. Do you take the time to simply just enjoy and celebrate? We put these thoughts into a poem:

> *When my days of hoops are done,*
> *I wish I might have one more run,*
> *a run that takes me from my stop*
> *to help others reach for the top.*

We hope you have appreciated the philosophies, structure, concepts, strategies, and reflections in this book. Perhaps a great program is best reflected in Coach John Wooden's statement:

> *"The main ingredient of a star*
> *is the rest of the team."*

TIME TO ACTIVATE

Concluding this book for future successes awaits you, the reader. We ask three questions and advise you to write down your responses. Think about your responses over the course of days and weeks, especially if you are preparing for next season. Reflection and evaluation take time for true thoroughness and self-definition.

    A. Where are you in your coaching career? Consider where you have been, what keeps you in coaching, and where you might see yourself in five years?

    B. After reading this book, in what new ways and in which areas within "P-R-O-G-R-A-M" do you see your coaching strengths and limitations? Can you identify two or three big ideas you are entertaining to employ in each category? For each one, evaluate why and how each of those particular concepts will make a positive difference in your program. Try to be as detailed as you can. We suggest you review the coaching evaluation you completed on page 3.

    C. Now, reread the book and take notes for those key ideas, or at the very least, find those parts for those key ideas and reread the concepts. We ask you to reread because like the commitment to coaching well, if the activity is worth the time, make the time worth it. In this way you will refresh your mind and see how the ideas will fit for the growth of your program. Plus, you will find provocative ideas you missed in your first reading.

THE FINAL FIVE

Al McGuire:
"Don't buy me flowers when I'm dead.
Buy me a drink when I'm alive."

Stated on a plaque in Philadelphia's Palestra:
"To play the game is great. To win the game is greater.
But to love the game is the greatest of all."

**Tanner Morgan, quarterback at the University of Minnesota,
after his team upset Penn State in a bowl game in 2019:**
"As an athlete and just in life, you should want pressure
because it means your life is significant."

Jim Calhoun (qtd. from *A Passion to Lead*):
"Talent determines what you can do in life.
Motivation determines what you're willing to do.
Attitude determines how well you will do it."

The Two Toms:
"Pressure makes diamonds."

Best of preparation to you.
Thank you for your attentiveness.

BIBLIOGRAPHY

Anstett, Tom. *Inside his Experienced Basketball Mind*. Now published. Willing and available for lectures, clinics, roundtables, book talks (etc.) at tomanstett23@gmail.com.

Auerbach, Red and Feinstein, John. *Let Me Tell You a Story*. New York: Little, Brown, and Company, 2004.

Austin, Jamey. *Does team chemistry actually exist? Ladders* in Apple News. 31 July 2020.

Basketball for Coaches: 7 Rebounding Drills. Online. 2020. https://www.basketball-forcoaches.com/rebounding-drills/.

Krzyzewski, Mike. *Leading With the Heart*. New York: Warner Books, 2000.

McCormack, Tom. *Inside his Prolific Basketball Mind*. Now published. Willing and available for lectures, clinics, roundtables, book talks (etc.) at tommccor-mack1125@gmail.com.

Riley, Pat. *The Winner Within*. New York: The Berkeley Publishing Group, 1993.

Robbins, Tony. https://selfmadesuccess.com/there-are-only-two-options-make-progress-or-make-excuses/.

Russell, Bill. *Russell Rules: 11 Lessons on Leadership from the Twentieth Century's Greatest Winner*. New York: Penguin, 2001.

Ryan, Bo (with Mike Lucas). *Another Hill to Climb*. Stevens Point: KCI Sports Publishing. 2008.

Stein, Alan. *Inspirational Stories from the NBA Players Top 100 Camp*. 23 August 2010. https://www.usab.com/youth/news/2010/08/inspirational-stories-from-the-nba-players-top-100-camp.aspx.

Ten Rules for Building a Business. 1 June 2020. https://corporate.walmart.com/our-story/history/10-rules-for-building-a-business.

Wooden, John and Jameson, Steve. *Wooden: a lifetime of observations and reflections on and off the court*. New York: Scribner, 1997.

ACKNOWLEDGMENTS

Thank you, Pat Sullivan, the former head men's basketball coach and assistant to the president at the University of St. Francis in Joliet, Illinois.
Your guidance was relevant and insightful. Pat has authored two books:
Attitude: the Cornerstone of Leadership and
Team Building: From the Bench to the Boardroom.
We highly recommend them for coaches and leaders.

(Personal from TA) Thank you, Tom McCormack.
Not only are you a fantastic person, coach, and friend, but also your insights and partnership made this venture worthwhile and enjoyable.

(Personal from TM) Thank you, Tom Anstett.
Your guidance and patience during the writing of this book goes beyond gratitude.
The same guidance and patience you showed when I was your assistant.
Thanks also for being such a great friend, coach, and teacher.

Thank you, Coach Bill Schaefer.
Your guidance, toughness, humor, and foresight assisted our journeys
in too many ways to count. We miss you and love you.

Thank you, Rick Majerus, Mike Krzyzewski, Hubie Brown, and many other coaches,
whose wisdom and generosity have helped us along the way.

Thank you to the coaches and professionals who took the time
to write testimonials for the book.

Thank you to the assistant coaches we have had the pleasure to know and to help us.

No coach succeeds without dedicated players.
Thank you to the players at the schools where we each coached.

ABOUT THE AUTHORS

TOM ANSTETT

Despite the first game he ever coached in 1973 going into four overtimes in a victory, Tom Anstett achieved over four decades of teaching and coaching. A Golden Apple nominee and two-time inductee (as a player in 2011 and as a coach in 2014) into the Illinois Basketball Coaches Hall of Fame are clear reflections of the passion and mastery of his craft.

Anstett played basketball at Boston College under the legendary (the late) Chuck Daly, then under Bob Zuffelato. After graduation, he began his teaching/coaching career in the Chicago area. He earned his MA in English Literature in 1989 and his administrative certification in 1997, both at Northeastern Illinois University. He was a head coach for 21 years (Immaculate Conception High School, Glenbrook North High School, and York High School) and an assistant at Lincoln-Way Central and East High Schools for fourteen. He was awarded District Coach of the Year three times. He also began a feeder program, the Frankfort Warriors, and ran that organization for seven years. While teaching English AP courses and College Writing and serving as the department chairman, Anstett published various poetry and English-related articles. He also has presented at several Illinois Association of Teachers of English conferences.

After retiring in 2014, Anstett wrote his first book, *Stop Whining; Start Winning: For Teachers and Coaches,* which was published in 2017. He still presents teacher workshops in English or Reading topics through the Joliet Professional Development Alliance in Joliet, Illinois. Anstett and his wife Susan have been married for 32 years, raising two sons, John and T.J. Anstett plays golf with varying success, instructs high school players in one-hour basketball lessons, exercises every day, reads daily, and enjoys family time. He currently lives in Green Bay, Wisconsin, near the company and wisdom of his two grandsons, Noah (5) and Rory (2).

TOM ANSTETT

(42 years):

Quigley Seminary-North, Chicago, IL—3

Immaculate Conception High School, Elmhurst, IL—8

Glenbrook North High School, Northbrook, IL—5

York Community High School, Elmhurst, IL—10

Lincoln-Way Central, North, and East High Schools, New Lenox and
Frankfort, IL—16

(While coaching at Lincoln-Way—the Frankfort Warriors feeder program
and traveling teams—7)

TOM McCORMACK

Fifty years ago, while playing on the DePaul University freshman basketball
team, Tom McCormack was asked to do a favor. His grade school, St. Genevieve,
needed an eighth-grade basketball coach. While going to school and playing
for the Blue Demons, he found the time to take his first coaching assignment.
The love affair began. Fifty years later McCormack answered a similar call for
the eighth-grade boys' team for Conant High School's feeder program.

McCormack earned a BA in Physical Education and an MA in Educational
Leadership at DePaul University. His basketball coaching stops included seven
years as an eighth-grade boys' coach at St. Genevieve and St. Athanasius,
ten years as a high school assistant boys' coach at all levels (Quigley North,
Immaculate Conception Catholic Prep), and 33 years as a high school boys'
head coach (Immaculate Conception and Conant). He was also an assistant
football coach for 43 years and filled in for the girls' varsity head coach at
I.C.C.P. at the end of one season.

Along the way have been numerous Coach of the Year awards from the Mid-Suburban League and the Illinois Basketball Coaches Association. McCormack was inducted into the I.B.C.A Hall of Fame as a coach in 2010 and ranks first all-time among Mid-Suburban League head boys' basketball coaches with 576 career victories.

McCormack retired from teaching in 2017 but still continues to give individual instruction in ballhandling and shooting to players of all ages. He lives in Schaumburg, Illinois, with his wife Mary. They have been married for 44 years and have four children: Patrick, Maureen, Matthew, and Kerry. Seven grandchildren spice his life. He likes to bike, still plays a little hoop, and spends time with family.

TOM McCORMACK

(50 years):
St Genevieve Grade School—2
Quigley Seminary-North, Chicago, IL—2
St. Athanasius Grade School, Evanston, IL—4
Immaculate Conception High School, Elmhurst, IL—7
Conant High School, Hoffman Estates, IL—32
Immaculate Conception, Elmhurst, IL—2
Conant 8th grade feeder team—1